dadcando

Published by Guardian Books 2010

2 4 6 8 10 9 7 5 3 1

First published in Great Britain in 2010 by
Guardian Books
Kings Place, 90 York Way
London N1 9GU

www.guardianbooks.co.uk

A CIP catalogue record for this book
is available from the British Library

ISBN 978-0852652015

Design by Two Associates

Printed and bound in China by C&C Offset Printing Co. Ltd

dadcando

Build, make, do ... the best way to
spend quality time with your kids

Chris Barnardo

gb

To India, James, William and Albie
with all my love, Dad xxx

bottle-cap beetle PAGE 31

contents

For printable designs and templates to enhance your dadcando projects, visit our dedicated microsite at:

www.guardianbooks.co.uk/dadcando

Introduction

What did you do at the weekend? It's a good question, and for many parents, their children are part of a weekend routine that they take for granted. Every week millions of mums and dads look forward to those two magic days (after a *long week*) as a time to relax, sleep in a bit or just have fun with their kids, without having to worry too much about work. But for dads who don't live with their children, 'The Weekend' develops a particular significance. If you're a separated dad, whether you see your children every week or only once a month, the time you spend together is at a premium, and what *you* did at the weekend takes on a meaning that only others in your position can really understand.

When you're a separated dad, weekends flicker past at a dizzying rate, as you try to make sure that every second counts. If you have been separated or divorced before, you know what to expect, and as a result you are better prepared. But what about the newly separated dad; the dad who wakes up one morning to find that he is on his own with his children to look after? How does he make sure that he continues to be a big part of his children's lives? How does he stop the stresses and strains of a painful separation spilling over into that precious time he spends with his children?

Research has shown that a father's role is critical to a developing child's ability to form relationships

In 2005 I started work building a specialist website aimed at helping dads get the most out of the time they spend with their children. The idea was to lend a hand on a practical level by sharing some of my experiences (hard-won through two divorces), to be a positive celebration of the father's role in his child's life, and to provide a creative resource as an inspiration for both dads and their children. I decided it was time that fathers celebrated their abilities, rather than focus too heavily on their problems. Research has shown that a father's role, and specifically the quality and sensitivity of play between a father and his children, is the most important factor in determining a growing child's ability to form and maintain normal relationships and feel secure in themselves[1]. So, because of the importance of play, I built the website around a core of original creative craft projects that I hoped would tap into a father's inner child, aligning it with the growing person inside his children. I called the site dadcando, since I firmly believe that a *dad **can** do* and does do so many vital things for his children. Dadcando is full of guidance, tips and positive strategies about how best to manage the extreme change that separation and divorce bring to a family. However, dadcando's goal of enriching the relationship between father and child is just as relevant to any busy dad who feels that he would like to get more out of the precious moments he is able spend with his children. This is because, as planned, dadcando revolves around an adventure into the creative mind of the child and the child in the heart of every dad.

William's pompom

We are children for only 20 per cent of our lives. It's a busy time too. We learn how to speak, we become self aware, we understand what it is to be loved and unloved. At different times we experience neglect, varying degrees of physical and emotional threat (such as bullying or punishment), and we learn how to live as an individual. Unfortunately it is likely that by the time we leave home, we will also have gone through our first divorce; obviously not our own, but that of the two people who mean everything to us, our mum and dad. When divorce strikes, suddenly the binary star at the centre of our solar system is frighteningly out of control, shattering our world and messing up our day and night. Our parents are not only our protectors and carers but also our most important role models. How we see them dealing with difficult situations, working through the fallout from arguments or coping with the stress of separation and divorce, starts a tape running in our head that plays back over and over throughout the rest of our lives, shaping our own behaviours and personal relationships.

Painful and difficult times are often referred to as 'character building' for the very reason that our survival as a species is dependent on us being able to learn from traumatic experiences and avoid them in the future. As a result, distressing experiences form very strong memories. It follows, therefore, that there is almost no more important time for the significance of both parents' roles to be evident than in the early weeks, months and years post-separation. This is when every member of the family is dealing with a range of damaging emotions and significant changes in their day-to-day lives, and our children are learning lessons about how they will deal with difficulties as adults.

It's obvious that nobody fares well when a family is broken up. The legal system does its best to formalise the role of separated mother and father under the premise of protecting the interests of the children, but the actual outcome is often highly unbalanced. In the end it is the children who then suffer as they are made to fit the relationship they used to have with one half of their parents into what can feel like snatched moments. As likely as not, these are dominated by stress, arguments and misguided one-upmanship.

At many times throughout history when sections of society have felt that they were being treated unjustly, they have risen up and attempted to change the situation, by force if necessary. The last decade has seen a concerted effort on the part of a few men to change what they see as the marginalisation of the father's vital role in the care of his children throughout their childhood, notwithstanding their separation and divorce from their children's mother. Ardent campaigners have become frustrated at the apparent lack of judicial progress. As they scale prominent buildings in demonstration to make their cause public, it's no surprise that they have come across as reactionary and sometimes even aggressive. While successful in raising awareness of the dreadful situation, these measures have at times been counterproductive to the cause. Extreme behaviour only serves to reinforce stereotypical views about gender roles and brings into question the suitability of men to the role of childcare.

It doesn't take a great leap of imagination to see the similarity of this painful struggle with the long-running campaign by suffragettes to secure women's voting rights at the turn of the 20th century. At that time a degree of now famous antisocial behaviour was necessary to attract the attention of a parliament

> **Our parents are not only our protectors and carers but also our most important role models**

Albie's submarine

that was happy to turn a blind eye to the complete absence of women's fundamental rights to participate equally in society.

Research carried out by psychologists and academics has shown that one of the most important factors in the long-term emotional wellbeing of a child of divorced parents is their relationship with the non-resident parent[2, 3]. Of course, in over 90 per cent of cases, this is the father. Despite the fact that today married British fathers undertake nearly half of all childcare[4], separated dads are still waiting for equality. The situation is improving, and although it has been 20 long years since the 1989 Children Act was meant to have made everything better, the legal system is finally starting to reflect the change in society.

James' peg chameleon

Dadcando's junk building projects are proof of the basic principle that good things can be made out of broken things; it's an analogy that cannot be lost on anyone in a separated family. Making things from scratch (called scratch building by model makers), from bits and pieces of old packaging lying around the house, practically demonstrates that things can be put together in many different ways. For the separated dad and child, dadcando's craft and model-making projects provide a focus for time spent together, and the finished item reinforces the joint experience. It will stick around as a constant reminder of the good times spent together as well as being a toy that will give hours of entertainment. Dadcando projects enable the father to re-learn how to be with his children, and by keeping his eyes and ears open, he gets to understand at a fundamental level

how his children think and feel in a way that is hard to better.

Yet making things together goes much further than the immediate satisfaction of the finished model. The lessons that are learned by solving all the problems that building something from scratch presents, translate extremely well into everyday life.

Problem solving is an important life skill and in my view, the key to happiness. Dadcando teaches it in a very subtle way. Each craft project provides an opportunity for practising problem-solving skills in a safe environment, which will have a hugely beneficial effect on how the projecteer perceives and then starts to tackle the bigger challenges in their lives. The projects are designed to appeal to children and parents alike, stretching abilities and developing both father and child's natural skills. The clear project plans don't diminish the need for creativity or problem solving on the part of the dad and child, because everyone's starting materials are slightly different and many small issues must be creatively solved if the task is to be completed. The plans form an outline of the tried and tested route for any given project from start to finish, merely making each one manageable and acting as a framework to give the novice builders confidence to tackle projects that they might otherwise never try.

Developing our creativity is important, because it is the engine that powers our problem-solving ability. Creativity is not an innate gift that only a lucky few have, we are all born with it and tapping back into our intrinsic creativity is a skill anyone can master.

Becoming creative is a two-step process. The first step is simply to start seeing the world differently to how you have learned to see it. Some may argue that creativity is actually seeing the world as

dadcando develops problem-solving skills which in my view are the key to happiness

India's pelican sketch

it really is, not just how we *think* it is. Once you can see the world as it really is, you become able to see all the options available to you, and you can put them together in new and exciting ways – this is the second part of the creative process. This is why creativity is key to problem solving. It's what lets you break out of the trap of going over the same solution time and time again, thinking that in doing so you might make it work even though you have failed that way 100 times before.

It's obvious really, in order to find new solutions to old problems, you have to think new thoughts. Creative people call thinking new thoughts, 'thinking outside-the-box'. The 'box' is the imaginary container that constrains our thinking and makes sure we always go down the same well-trodden paths. The box is what stops us thinking new thoughts and trying new ways of doing things. It's what causes us to make the same mistakes over and over again. Our parents helped us build our box out of our upbringing, and as we've grown up we have reinforced it to a bulletproof thickness with habits and surroundings that we're familiar with and don't really see any more. It's the glass ceiling that stops us soaring. It is the box that we are building for our children that will surely turn them into us.

Thinking outside-the-box is not difficult but you have to work at it, because the box is so intrinsically woven into the fabric of ourselves that it is difficult to know where to start, and it is hard to know when we are actually thinking outside-the-box. The 'Bucket Thought Experiment' illustrates the problem and its solution beautifully. Ask anyone to come up with as many uses for a bucket as they can. Tell them that you're aiming for 25 different ways of using a bucket. Typically you will get answers along the lines of: something to carry water in, a coal bucket, an ice bucket, or a vase, for example. At first glance it looks like a good start, but on review all these uses are the same one – a container. To think outside-the-box, you have to come up with *different* uses for the bucket. Some examples of different uses might be: a loudhailer (knock the bottom out), a small stepladder, a hat, a sandcastle maker, a weapon, or an *objet d'art*, for example.

Kids naturally do this sort of thing all the time, and as we re-learn how to think like this for ourselves, we not only start to see new ways of getting round old problems but we also start to understand our children so much better. Once you can look at a bottle top and see a pair of dragon hunter's goggles, or hold a toothbrush and imagine a fighter plane wingtip, then you are starting to get the idea. You will find that this fresh way of thinking brings out the positive aspects of the child inside you, has a dramatic effect on the way you think about lots of things, and most importantly of all, helps you get the most out of the time you spend with your kids.

Here's to new and happy times being a dad that does.

Thinking outside-the-box is not difficult, but it does take practice.

1. K. Grossmann *et al*, **The Uniqueness of the Child-Father Attachment Relationship: Fathers' Sensitive and Challenging Play as a Pivotal Variable in a 16-year Longitudinal Study**, Social Development, Volume 11, Number 3, July 2002, pp. 301-337(37), Blackwell Publishing

2. J Dunn *et al*, **Children's perspectives on their relationships with their non-resident fathers: Influences, outcomes and implications**, Journal of Child Psychology and Psychiatry (2004) 45(3) 553.

3. J Sturge & D Glaser, **Contact and Domestic Violence – The Experts Court Report (2000)**, Family Law 615, at p.617

4. An Equal Opportunities Commission (EOC) study conducted in 2007 reported that fathers now look after their children for an average of two and a quarter hours per day, only quarter of an hour less than the mother's average of two and a half hours.

BEFORE YOU START

In this book you'll discover loads of exciting making and doing projects. For some you'll only need five minutes, with others, whole afternoons will dissolve away. Some require just a piece of paper, while for others you'll need old packaging junk and a few bits of basic making equipment. Some models are easy to put together, whereas others will help you and your children develop more advanced scratch building skills.

Whichever projects you choose, you'll find that the instructions have been carefully designed to be very clear, and the finished product is cheap to make. For the most part, the bits you'll need to make the model cost nothing, or are free bits of rubbish that you would normally throw away!

The projects here are completely original, fun and relevant to kids, and have been designed with you in mind. Quick and easy with really satisfying results, they ensure that even when time is short you can get the most out of the moments you and your children have together. Making and doing things with your kids is about giving them the most valuable thing you can give them – your time. Our 'making' projects are about solving problems together and having something at the end that your child can keep, play with and feel proud of. Anything you make with your children will be very special to them because you spent the time together making it.

Most of the instructions come with templates or patterns that you can trace over to ensure that all the models you make look as good as they possibly can. But before you start, here's some information and advice on the tools and equipment you will need for the more involved projects.

Craft knives

While scissors are much safer, and you should use those when you can, there will come a time when you have to use a knife to cut something out. We are assuming that you know how to use a knife carefully. Most model-makers have a few 'battle scars' from slips made with very sharp knives when they were rushing, tired or not paying attention. However, if you are careful, cutting something out with the right knife will give you a very good finish.

Always use the right knife for the job

Craft knives come in a wide range of different shapes and sizes, but the most useful are the Stanley knife and the scalpel. For jobs that don't require fine detail and are too tough for a scalpel, the utility or box-cutter knife (commonly known as a Stanley

knife, after the company that first manufactured it in volume) is very handy. The smaller craft knife, which has a long blade that can be snapped off at intervals to keep it sharp, is also useful, but if you have a Stanley knife and a scalpel then you have most things covered. The design of most craft knives allows the blade to be retractable for safe storage, but even so, these pieces of equipment should always be stored somewhere out of the reach of your children.

Sharp knives should never be used by children, and you should be careful when using them. You can teach your kids a great deal about responsible use of equipment by setting a good example when you use a knife to cut out something for them.

SAFETY FIRST

A Stanley knife will make short work of most forms of packaging, and the vase project on p22 was made in about 20 minutes just by slicing up a couple of empty plastic bottles.

When planning what to cut, it's best to draw on the surface using a thin permanent marker so that you can make a neat incision in the right place. To draw a straight line around the base of a bottle, hold it with the end to be cut in the palm of the hand you write with, while holding the marker. Press the marker against the bottle where you want to cut it and draw round the bottle by revolving it without moving the pen. That way you will get a nice horizontal line. Take care when cutting the necks of bottles, as these are the thickest parts and are often impossible to cut with any knife. The best way to cut through the neck of a plastic bottle is with a junior hacksaw. Using a junior hacksaw is safe for kids because the saw teeth are very small, and it's a fun way to teach them how to use a saw.

Scalpel

The scalpel deserves a special mention here because it is the cutting tool of choice for the graphics and model-making industry. Typically, craft knives are differentiated from other knives because they have removable, disposable blades that allow you to keep them as sharp as possible. There are a huge number of different-shaped blades and handles available, so it is easy to get confused, but it does make the scalpel one of the most flexible knives.

Each blade type has a number, as does each handle variant. For model-making you only need one blade shape, and that's number 10A. (Note: do not get a number 10 as this type has a curved blade edge and is very difficult – dangerous even – to cut with against a ruler). The handle variant to go for is handle number 3. Change the blade regularly so that it stays sharp and you don't have to press too hard when cutting. If the material you are working with is thick or tough, then use a stronger craft knife rather than risk pressing so firmly that you snap the scalpel blade. The blades are sold singly, in little foil packs of five, or in boxes of 100. However, a box of 100 bought online only costs twice as much as a pack of five bought in my local art shop, so as with anything, it is most definitely worth buying in bulk.

Scalpel blades are extremely sharp and are perfect for cutting foamboard, thin card or paper so that the edges are really neat. As with any blade, scalpels should be handled with care and children should **SAFETY FIRST** never be allowed to use them. That is definitely a job for Dad or Mum. Be careful when changing the blade because it is easy to slip, and take care when model-making. Always put the tool out of the reach of your children when using it and after use, remove the blade and put it back in its packaging so that it doesn't jab you when you're rummaging around in the kitchen drawer later on.

TIP: Because of its very fine point, a scalpel is perfect for cutting round small details. But remember, the blade is so sharp that it will cut through more than just the layer you want to cut, so always work on a surface where it won't matter if it gets marked.

A very sharp knife, traditionally used by surgeons, that's great for cutting out detail in relatively thin materials

Any piece of thick cardboard will do for a makeshift cutting mat and most graphic designers resort to using the back of their drawing pads in an emergency. However, a self-healing cutting mat is probably a wise investment; it extends the life of your blades, makes cutting more controllable (it slows the blade down as you cut with it) and will save you making horrendous marks and scratches in your kitchen tabletop.

To bend foamboard, cut a V-shaped groove in one side, being careful not to cut all the way through, and then fold. If you want a really strong fold, run a line of glue-gun glue along the bottom of the V-shaped groove before bending it into shape.

Foamboard

Also called polyboard or foamcore, foamboard is a wonderfully light, yet rigid, cardboard 3mm to 5mm thick, made from sandwiching a layer of Styrofoam between two sheets of thin, high-quality card. It's really easy to cut and folds to give clean, professional-looking bends.

> **A fabulous material for making structural models very quickly, it's lightweight and bends and cuts beautifully**

The glue gun works a treat on foamboard, so you can quickly knock together some impressive models with it. It is a very rewarding material to use because finished models are robust and the excellent surface will take a range of paint finishes, from markers to emulsion and spray paint. Kids love this board and it's great for creating something special for homework or to take into school. The most useful size to go for is probably 5mm thick, A2, which will cover you for practically every project.

Of course you shouldn't write off other types of board. We are bombarded with packaging these days and it is generally made from a wide range of engineering-quality materials. The sides of plastic washing-powder bottles are thin sheets of polyethylene (PE) or polypropylene (PP), and fruit juice cartons are usually waxed or PE-coated and foil-lined medium weight card – cut one open and look inside. These materials look great when used on a model. For small flexible sheets try cutting open an old toothpaste tube; many of them are made from multilayer barrier plastics with a foil lining, and that's magic stuff for putting the finishing touches to a range of great models.

Different types of cardboard

Thin, lightweight card from breakfast cereal packaging or a craft shop, is useful for small models and surface finishing touches. Can be bent and cut easily with scissors.

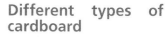

Thick pulp board is the sort you find on the back of a sketching pad. Good strength, but difficult to cut or bend. You will need a craft knife and to be very careful when cutting.

Corrugated or fluted packing board is readily available at your local supermarket, where they throw away tonnes of cardboard boxes. Can be strong, bends well one way (along the flutes), and is reasonably easy to cut using a knife or strong scissors. It also glues well with a glue gun.

Medium thickness foamboard is quite expensive at about £3 (do a web search for the cheapest and buy it online) and you will need sharp knives for cutting it, but this board cuts, folds and glues with a glue gun very nicely. It can be difficult to get radius bends, though.

Polymorph

I stumbled across Polymorph in the Maplin catalogue and thought it might come in handy for something or other. Composed of plastic chips that soften in hot water at about 60°C, it can be moulded by hand before setting rock hard, so it's great for moulding small components like robot hands, doll or puppet faces, or dolls' house items, for example. It's a plastic with a very low melting point that sets as tough as polypropylene and is almost indestructible when it's set. A useful quantity (250g), in granule form, only costs about £10, and when you want to use it you just put the granules in a jug and pour boiling water over them. After about two minutes in the hot water, the granules, which start out opaque white, go transparent and start to agglomerate and soften. Once it's transparent, you pour the water away – none of it gets absorbed – and the lump of plastic can be taken from the jug and moulded into any shape you like. When hot, Polymorph is very malleable and yet it is just about cool enough to manipulate with your bare hands. However, younger children should not be allowed to handle the hot plastic, and young people of 12 years and over will still need some supervision.

The hot plastic is easy to form and holds its shape reasonably well while it is setting. However, it is not an ideal modelling clay because there is a degree of elasticity to its behaviour, rather than it being perfectly plastic. Nevertheless, the brilliant thing about Polymorph is that within a few minutes, as it cools, it quickly hardens into

> **A hot-water softening plastic that sets rock hard in minutes, great for moulding little details for your models**

a very tough, rigid white plastic that is completely reusable. If you are not happy with the result, simply return it to the hot water and it softens again.

The product specification and instructions claim that you can machine the hardened plastic but I would beg to differ on this point. The average person's home machining tools are not water-cooled, and so typical equipment like electric drills and jigsaws will generate so much heat from friction that the material rapidly goes over its softening point and it therefore becomes impossible to get a good finish. In addition to that, it's far too tough to carve with a knife when it is set. In fact, attempting to do so could be very dangerous if the piece is not held down properly, because it is very slippery. My advice is to use Polymorph to make selected components within your model and aim to make them entirely by moulding them in the few minutes of soft-time you have after you have heated the material. Once you are happy with the result, the hardened material can be coloured in using permanent markers, or painted with acrylic or spray paint.

Double-sided sticky tape

There are loads of different types of sticky tape available, but when model-making or doing crafts, none is quite as useful as double-sided sticky tape. Double-sided sticky tape is a very thin plastic tape coated with an open adhesive on both sides and

is supplied rolled up and stuck on to a non-stick release paper. It provides very quick, clean and relatively strong sticking power for card, paper and board. Children can use it without getting into a gluey mess and the results are very neat.

Cut small squares of tape and use them as little sticky pads for holding paper in place in frames, or when folded up. Stick it to the back of things before you cut them out so that you make sure you have edge-to-edge adhesive. Use it in place of wet glue or a glue stick to make envelopes for a really strong finish.

Double-sided sticky tape is great for wrapping presents up neatly because you put the tape on the underside of the paper and don't spoil the wrapping paper you've used.

Get your children to draw their own stickers and then put double-sided tape on the back of the paper and cut the stickers out with a pair of kitchen scissors. They can then peel off the backing whenever they want and use the stickers they've made.

Wet glues

There are a range of glues available for use in the home. Poly-vinyl acetate or PVA glue (also referred to as white glue or wood glue) is a tough rubbery polymer. Your kids will be familiar with PVA because it is used extensively in schools. From a model-making point of view nothing is a substitute for the power and speed of a glue gun – so in my house the PVA glue tends to stay in the cupboard. Nevertheless, it's still a superb wood glue, where the water-based glue vehicle can really wet out the surface and soak

One of the best ways to stick paper and card together strongly and neatly with no mess

Choose the right glue for the right job, otherwise you will waste a lot of time waiting for things to dry

into the wood, to create a joint that is often stronger than the surrounding wood. The trouble with PVA is that it is not good at sticking polythene or polypropylene, which are the two most common packaging plastics, and materials that are used in quite a few of the models in this book. It also takes ages to dry, which means that kids can lose interest in the project or have to wait overnight to see the results of their handiwork.

However, PVA works brilliantly for papier-mâché projects. Just water it down a bit, no more than half and half water, and pour the glue on to a dinner plate so the paper can be soaked through more easily. A mixture of newspaper and absorbent kitchen roll torn into strips or crumpled up into balls provides quick bulk for papier-mâché.

Doing a project like this will be great fun and very messy, so although most PVAs are washable, your kids shouldn't be in their Sunday best when they are getting glue all over themselves. Don't bother buying tiny little bottles of PVA, go to a builders' merchants and buy a 2.5 litre bottle of PVA Bonding. It's basically exactly the same as the expensive wood glue, but it's a fraction of the price. If you want a handy pack to use round the house or on little paper projects, just decant some of it into an old shampoo bottle, but remember to write on the bottle what it is in permanent marker or someone who doesn't know what you've done could be heading for one gloopy hairdo!

Glue sticks and two-part resins are OK but not as useful as Spray Mount and a glue gun, which, respectively, replace them. Glue sticks tend to be lumpy, although they do have the advantage of being easy and safe for a child to use. Two-part resins are very strong, but they take time to cure, can be very messy and do not stick packaging plastics together that well. Once they are mixed they are very liquid and for many jobs you might have trouble keeping the glue exactly where you want it. For just about every model-making project where a two-part resin could be used, glue-gun glue will work better and is easier to use.

Superglue (cyanoacrylate) is very good at sticking skin together – there are medical grades approved for closing wounds –and great care must be taken when using it. **SAFETY FIRST** Children should never be allowed to use superglue. It sticks vinyl (PVC) together very well, so is useful for mending most types of blow-up beach toys (use an old vinyl tax disc holder or window sticker as the patch), but is not suitable for most model and toy-making projects because it is so thin, and it's designed to stick broken surfaces together only when they match perfectly.

Spray glue

Spray glue (also called by its leading brand name, Spray Mount) is what started me thinking about the availability of performance glues and proper 'making stuff' for kids to use, just like grown-ups. In the graphics industry Spray Mount replaced Cow Gum as a rapid-fix glue for sticking sheet materials together.

Once you have used spray glue you are unlikely to ever go back to any other form of wet glue for sticking sheets of paper or card together. A light dusting is all that's needed to fix things like photos in place, and, yes, it's the glue they use in those kids' TV art programmes when they've finished a picture and magically place it on a background where it stays. No wrinkling up at the edges, no wet patches, and if you stick your picture down in the wrong place or slightly wonky, then on most surfaces it is repositionable for the first few minutes.

Simply the best way to stick sheets of paper or card to each other

As with any aerosol, kids should not be allowed to use this glue unsupervised. Remember, as it's a spray, the glue will get everywhere. When you use it, make sure you read the instructions and only do **SAFETY FIRST** so in a ventilated room. Spray on to a surface that you don't mind getting glue on – usually that means putting down loads of newspaper, even more than you would think!

There is a knack to using this adhesive though, and if you are not careful you can end up covering other things with over-sprayed glue. This can be a problem as it is very sticky and hard to remove without using an artist's spirit-based cleaning solvent. Your best bet is to lay the piece to be covered in glue upside-down in the middle of a large piece of old newspaper and make sure you don't spray on to the surrounding area.

We use spray glue to stick all manner of templates and printed paper to anything flat that needs decorating. It is ideal for sticking things like photos, tickets and news cuttings neatly into a scrapbook.

Glue gun

No home is complete without a glue gun. Yes, it sounds like a bold statement. You may also think it a bit excessive of me to claim that it is one of the best inventions of the 20th century, if not of all time. I know that the best invention was the printing press, but the glue gun has the power to unlock your children's imagination and allow you and them to make things out of old junk as quickly as you want. Who knows how many future inventors, entrepreneurs, and professors were set on the road to greatness by something as humble as the glue gun?

So, what is it? The glue gun is a device for melting a thermoplastic resin glue, usually in the form of a long milky coloured stick about 10mm in diameter. The glue is extremely tough when set, and because it typically takes less than a minute to harden, it is perfect for instantaneous, high-performance sticking when making things. In fact I would say that if you have a glue gun, permanent marker and some old discarded packaging, you have almost everything you need to start making something good right away.

There are both low and high temperature versions of the glue gun, but as even the low

One of the greatest inventions ever and you can buy one for around £10!

temperature ones can reach 100°C and cause nasty burns, so care should be taken when using either type. Children should be supervised at all times, even if they have used them before.

The great thing about a glue gun when making things is that it will stick almost any object or surface to any other and can even be used to backfill cracks and gaps.

A glue gun will only cost about £10 and can be bought online or in any DIY store. Once you have one, you'll find that its usefulness extends far beyond these projects into fixing all manner of things around the home. I'd recommend that you get an extra packet of sticks when you buy your glue gun as they can get used up quite quickly.

I know I keep saying it, but ... glue guns and melted glue get very hot indeed and the glue is also very sticky. Children should not be allowed to use a glue gun unsupervised and if they are using it under supervision they need to be shown which bits heat up and learn how to use the gun without getting the hot melted glue on their fingers. If a burn does occur, get the glue off the skin as quickly as possible and run the burned area under cold water for at least five minutes. Turn your glue gun off after using it and put it to the back of the work surface out of reach while it cools down. Make sure the wire isn't trailing anywhere where it might get tripped over.

 SAFETY FIRST

Paint

You don't have to use paint to finish off your models, but it can make a big difference to the overall look.

Not all models really need paint, but items made from objects with writing or labels on them will look about a million times better if the lettering is covered up. In the case of the Space Rocket (p164) we used white paper wrapped round a crisps tube and a toilet roll to give us the nice white finish, which we could then use marker on without getting our fingers wet.

For the Floating Submarine (p97), black and grey spray paint transformed it in about two minutes from a couple of old plastic bottles into something really exciting that remained a favourite bathtime toy for months.

You can use any type of spray paint, but be careful to follow the instructions on the can. The paint is flammable when being sprayed, is bad for you if you breathe in the fumes and leaves a strong smell in your house for days. On the other hand, spray paint is ideal for quickly and permanently covering plastic, and spray paint for craft applications comes in a range of exciting finishes.

Use spray paint or emulsion for a quick finish that covers almost anything really well

For quick coverage on most surfaces you can do a lot worse than standard, house decorating emulsion. If you don't have any left over from your own DIY projects then you can buy tiny cans of paint, also known as match pots, very cheaply. Emulsion is better for covering cardboard quickly and the beauty of it is that you can wash the brushes in water. Be careful of clothes though, emulsion dries in about two minutes and thereafter is impossible to remove.

canoe PAGE 109

Acrylic paint is also very good at covering lettering up and sticking to most surfaces, and although it is water-based, it has the benefit of being permanent – rather than water-soluble – when it's dry. Acrylic paints dry very quickly and give bright satisfying colours, and they can also be used to tint emulsion. Tubes of acrylic are reasonably expensive, but they are lovely to use and the colours in them can all be mixed together to give a very professional finish. Acrylic paint also comes in big bottles which are much cheaper and can be picked up at most good toy shops or online.

Permanent markers

Surface decoration really makes a difference to the look of your models. You can paint them with emulsion or spray, but a very quick way to finish them off is by drawing on them with a permanent marker. Permanent markers can stain, so be careful with your clothes.

A very quick way to let your kids personalise your models, giving them detail and character

The best marker to have for most uses is the bulletpoint type, like the medium one shown here. It's also useful to have a thinner one – the type of marker you use to write on CDs or overhead projector film is ideal. And of course, because you want things to be fun, why not get a huge jumbo marker? They're not expensive and the kids always have fun colouring in using such a big pen and loads of black ink! Markers are perfect for adding names and little details to models that you have sprayed or painted over all in one colour. Always write something on your models, it is an important finishing step. Let your kids name the model and/or think up and design imaginary organisations and logos. If the model needs a number, then why not use a number special to them, their age or their favourite number? Play is all about buying into the fantasy and these finishing touches and little ways of personalising your homemade model add a huge

amount of playability. Don't forget that permanent markers now come in gold and silver and can be used to colour a whole range of cardboards and plastics to give a bright, metallic finish, instantly.

Before you actually put pen to model, type out what you want to write on your model using your computer. Type at the right size and use a font style that you like or is particularly suitable, the NASA font for spaceships, or a stencil font for hardware, for example. Then, using the typed letters as a reference, copy the text on to the model using the marker. You could also look for reference images of real versions of your model and copy their sponsorship and logos – you'll be surprised at the difference a few carefully placed graphics will make.

The canoe opposite only took about 30 minutes to make. It's not painted, but it is completely transformed by the name drawn on to it.

Putting LEDs into your models

LEDs (light emitting diodes) are brilliant for adding an extra twinkle to your model. They are low power, low current drain (meaning that they last a long time on the same battery) and they can be very bright and small, so you can put them almost anywhere in a model or homemade toy. They are also very cheap.

> To add the finishing touches to an advanced model, nothing works better than a bit of light

A very quick and easy way to introduce an LED light to your model is to use the guts from a cheap keyring or pen light torch. You can use the torch exactly as is, just putting the whole thing in the model and arranging it so the button is easily accessible, or pressed on by an extra bit of cardboard. As those little pen torches only cost a few pence, you can afford to put them in every model.

If you have some thin wire, separate the LED from the switch battery assembly so that you can mount the LED anywhere on the model and have the battery and switch unobtrusively somewhere else. Break open the keyring light housing and wrap one end of each of the thin wires round the LED legs and sticky-tape the other end of the wires to the battery / switch assembly. Take care that the polarity is the same as it was before, because the LED will not work and may be damaged if connected the wrong way across a battery.

On the web you will find a massive range of very cheap LEDs for sale by mail order. Choose the hyper-bright flashing ones that have a built-in resistor, so that they can be wired straight to a 9V battery without the need for any other components. You can use solder if you have a soldering iron, but wrapping wire tightly round the LED legs and sticking with tape is just as good for a model. A battery connector is useful for the battery end of the wires because the positive terminal of a PP3 9V is very hard to wrap a wire round. If you have designed a toy or model so that the LED is only switched on while it is being played with, a 9V PP3 battery will last the lifetime of the model and can be sealed up inside. This saves the complication of having to build a removable panel to change the battery.

happy making!

I have found the best way to give advice to your children is to find out what they want, and then advise them to do it.

HARRY S TRUMAN
33rd president of the United States

EASY PROJECTS

fluffy ladybird PAGE 37

space vase PAGE 22

FELT-PEN CHROMATOGRAPHY

being there
WHEN IT REALLY MATTERS

52

fish doorhandles PAGE 45

space vase

Make a vase for real flowers – in minutes!

7 years +

20 minutes

Plastic bottles
Glue gun
Kitchen scissors
Craft knife

This is a fabulously simple project and a great one to get you going on the whole making-stuff thing. All you need are two old plastic bottles and you're on your way. For this one we used a family-sized smoothie bottle for the base and a conditioner bottle for the flower holder. Given that these vases are so simple to make, why not put together a few and paint them in as many different ways are there are colours in the rainbow? The vase makes a great holder for the spooky flowers on p24 and, as it holds water when finished, it's perfect for cut flowers too.

space vase

GLUE

1 Take two plastic bottles, for haircare products or drinks, one long and slender, the other wide.

2 Keep the cap from the thin bottle but cut its base off. To do this neatly, first mark a ring where you are going to cut, using a permanent marker.

3 Cut the shoulder portion from the wide bottle, removing the neck and all the body.

4 Glue the lid on to the thin bottle, invert it and glue it into the open neck of the wide bottle. For the best effect use a glue gun.

5 Paint, ideally using spray paint, although house emulsion might work if mixed with a single drop of washing-up detergent.

Turn over the page to make some stunning flowers to display.

spooky flowers

Pompom blossoms from a plastic bag

12 years +

40 minutes

A4 paper sheet
Double-sided tape
White glue
Card
Bin liner
Glue gun
Kitchen scissors
Paint

These flowers are wonderfully easy to make and you don't even need wool. The pompoms are made from plastic and can be any colour you want, but for a really eerie feel, why not try black bin liners? The stems are made from a rolled-up piece of printer paper, and are a modern version of papier-mâché. The paper is rolled and glued using a coating of PVA glue to give a durable, woodlike stalk and the stem is decorated with glue-gun glue to give long, delicate surface features. The whole lot is then painted black or silver (spray-paint is best), with the raised features highlighted in a bright contrasting colour so that they glow against the dark paint. When you glue this stem into the black plastic pompom head the end result is a beautiful table or window decoration.

The instructions here include a template sheet to trace over and help you make the pompom discs the perfect size.

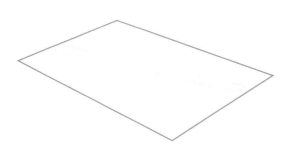

1 Stick a strip of double-sided tape diagonally across a sheet of A4 paper.

4 (OPTIONAL) When the glue is dry, using the glue gun, make three stripes along the stem to give it an organic form.

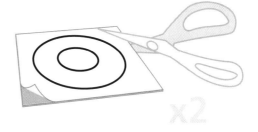

2 Roll the paper up very tightly diagonally so that you have a thin rolled-up stem shape.

5 Paint the stem black or silver with a paint that dries waterproof (spray or acrylic are ideal).

6 When the paint is dry, paint the glue-gun strips in a very bright dayglo colour or even glow-in-the-dark paint.

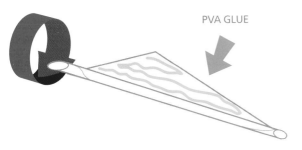

PVA GLUE

3 When you roll over the double-sided tape stop and put a little PVA on the remaining paper.

7 Trace over the template provided and cut out two discs of thick cardboard.

x2

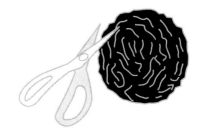

8 Cut a large black dustbin liner in half, top to bottom, and thread it through both discs, tightly wrapping it round and round.

11 Cut away the cardboard discs and trim to make a regular ball-shape pompom.

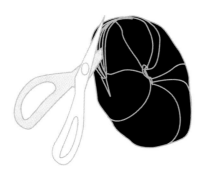

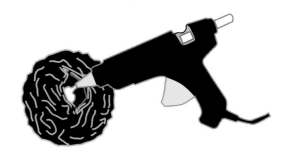

9 When you can't wrap any more round, slit the edge first with a craft knife and then with scissors.

12 Part the plastic folds and put some glue-gun glue at the centre of the pompom.

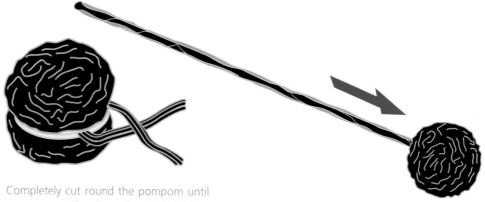

10 Completely cut round the pompom until you can see the discs, then tightly tie a piece of string or plastic bag (if you want to be able to recycle it later) round the middle to secure.

13 Poke the stem up into the pompom. Support until set.

spooky flowers

pompom disc TEMPLATE **x 2**

chocolate rice krispie cakes

Delicious treats you don't even need to bake

7 years +

15 mins to prepare,
20–30 mins to chill

Fork
Non-metallic mixing bowl
Crisps tube or drink bottle
Knife
Strong scissors
Mug

2 x 250g Bar of chocolate
Knob of butter
1.5 x Mug dry Rice Krispies
1tsp Sugar

This recipe is quick, easy and great fun to make – nothing beats the sweet smell of melting chocolate. As well as guiding you through the recipe, we'll also show you how to form your own cupcake holders, so really this is a cooking and making project in one. The chocolate can be milk, white or dark, just avoid using bars like Flake or Mars as they contain ingredients which stop them melting properly. The exact quantity of ingredients isn't really important, but you will need enough chocolate to coat the Rice Krispies and enough of the cereal to fill some or all of your homemade cake rings. The recipe here should make 12 cakes, so enough for 12 kids or one very hungry kid!

chocolate rice krispie cakes

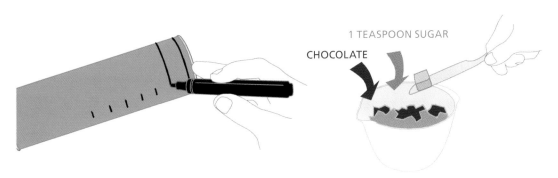

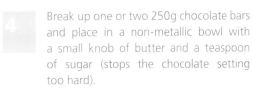

1 TEASPOON SUGAR

CHOCOLATE

1 The idea is that you don't need cup cake holders here, all you need is some little discs. So take either a crisp tube or a small drink bottle and mark it off at roughly 15mm intervals and then draw lines to the marks making sure that they are neat.

4 Break up one or two 250g chocolate bars and place in a non-metallic bowl with a small knob of butter and a teaspoon of sugar (stops the chocolate setting too hard).

2 Make the initial cut with a craft or kitchen knife and then cut out the rings with strong kitchen scissors.

5 Microwave the chocolate, butter, sugar mix on medium for about 10 seconds at a time, stirring between each burst, until the chocolate is melted and the butter and sugar are mixed in.

RICE KRISPIES

RICE KRISPIES

3 You don't need baking paper – just lay a couple of sheets of plain paper on a suitable tray or flat surface and place the rings on that.

6 Gently stir the Rice Krispies into the melted mixture, trying not to crush too many.

▶

7 Spoon the chocolate-covered Rice Krispies into the rings, then pat them down gently with the back of the spoon so that they are nice and flat.

8 Chill in the fridge for about 30 minutes then press out.

While they are setting why not make some wizard's sweet and cake boxes on p192?

bottle-cap beetle

Lyra had one chasing her, AA Milne had one called Alexander and Volkswagen made 21 million of them. Now you can make your own beetle from bottle caps in just a few minutes with this great little project designed by Jellyfishguy, a dadcando website member.

It's hard to believe how cool this beetle looks when you know that it is just three different-sized bottle caps. You need a tiny little toothpaste tube cap or flip lid for the head, a fizzy drink bottle lid or similar for the body, and a larger, flatter lid like the one that comes off a one- to four-litre milk bottle, for the carapace. Spray yours black like we have or make a fancy version with magical powers by spraying it gold and decorating it with runes.

To make your beetle, simply trace our leg and wing templates and follow these easy instructions.

A wicked-looking beetle made from junk

8 years +

30 minutes

Glue gun
  or fast resin glue
Black paint
Paper clips
Plastic bottle caps
Plastic food tray
Clear plastic
  packaging

1 Take one small plastic bottle cap from either a drink bottle or a household cleaner bottle, rest it on a piece of card and draw round it with a permanent marker.

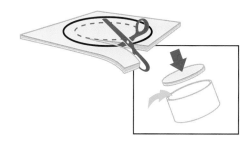

2 Cut out a smaller disc of card to fit inside the bottle cap using the line you drew as a guide, and glue into the underside of the cap, flush with the bottom.

LEG TEMPLATE

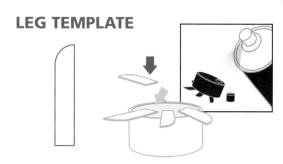

3 Trace the template, then cut out six legs from a thin plastic food tray and glue three poking out from the bottom of the cap. Spray or paint the cap and a small toothpaste tube cap black.

WING TEMPLATE

4 Trace the template, then cut out four wing shapes from a piece of clear plastic packaging, draw two or three thin black lines on the wings and then stick them on to the top of the cap as shown.

5 To make the head, glue the toothpaste tube lid on to the side of the bottle cap, opposite the wings.

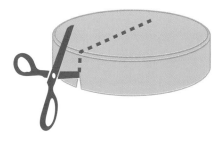

6 To make the carapace, using strong scissors cut a larger, flatter, soft bottle cap up one side and across most of the top. Use a milk poly-bottle cap or similar.

7 Using the scissors, cut a semicircle that is a little bit larger than the toothpaste tube cap out of the larger cap's side, then pull apart the two sides of the cap.

9 Stick the carapace to the body of the beetle so that it is up at an angle (use glue-gun glue) and hold the carapace in place until it is set. For the antennae, bend two paper clips and glue into the head.

8 Spray or paint the carapace.

Does your beetle need some company? Go to p37 and make a ladybird to join him.

string nest

This isn't a string vest ... it's a string nest

8 years +

1 hour (plus drying)

String
Balloon
White glue

download available

If glue and paper is called papier-mâché, then perhaps this method could be called 'corde mâché', corde being the French word for string. String and white glue is a great craft combination. String is pliable and easy to drape round things when it is wet with PVA glue, but yet it dries hard and solid and is easy to paint. Building this nest makes a nice, satisfying mess so you'll need to be wearing aprons or old clothes with your sleeves rolled up and have lots of newspaper to put down.

Use a non-toxic paint to paint the nest, and preferably one that dries waterproof – spray paint is ideal. Then fill the nest with bits of cotton wool and decorate the underside with leaves cut from green felt. If you are worried about the paint coming off on the eggs, simply fill your nest with little foil-wrapped ones. The end result makes a beautiful present.

string nest

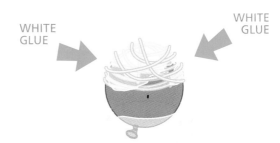

WHITE
GLUE

WHITE
GLUE

1 Partially blow up a small balloon so that it is only about 10cm in diameter.

4 Cover with more white glue and start to wind string round the balloon, making sure that the string is covered with glue.

2 Rest the balloon in a jug or vase to support it.

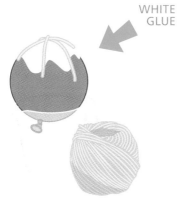

WHITE
GLUE

5 Wind more string round, adding glue as you do so that the string is wet, until you have covered about half of the balloon.

3 Cover the top of the balloon in white glue and lay some string pieces over the top. It helps to wet the string first in a mixture of water and white glue.

6 Allow to dry somewhere warm for 24 hours and then carefully remove the nest from the balloon.

▶

7 Paint or spray the nest dark brown (spray is certainly easier). If you want you could add pieces of cotton wool or green felt leaves.

8 Fill the nest with little foil wrapped eggs.

Visit our website to print gift tags you can colour in.

fluffy ladybird

Getting this terrific spotted effect on a pompom is surprisingly easy when you know how, and you can choose any two colours you like to make this little bug. Ladybirds come in all shades of red, orange and yellow, but why not have a go at making a bright blue or green one too?

As with the spooky flowers earlier in this chapter, you can use plastic bags to make these pompoms, so there's nothing to stop you getting going right away. Black, white or green bin liners work well, as do sandwich bags, which come in a range of subtle colours. As the ladybird's eyes are so small, when glueing them on use a tiny spot of glue-gun glue on the head and put the eye on to that. Be careful not to burn your fingers, and if you have a pin to hand, pick the eye up and position it with that.

Spotty wool – how will you do it?

7 years +

40 minutes

Wool (two colours)
Bottle cap
Paper clip
Cardboard
Detergent bottle
Bendy straws
Scissors
Glue gun
Beads

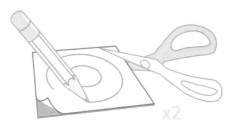

1 Trace two disc templates guides from the template on p40. Glue the disc guides to a thin piece of card and cut out two discs.

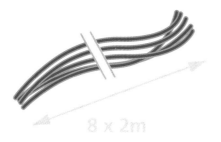

2 Prepare the wool by doubling it up so that you have pieces about 2m long in bundles of about six to ten strands, depending on how thick the wool is. You may need three or four such bundles.

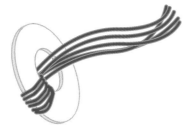

3 Starting with the body colour, pass the wool through the hole in the middle of the disc repeatedly so that you wind it round the disc, until you have just covered it completely.

4 To make the spots, wind the spot colour wool bundle only twice through in one place, and then, leaving a gap, do the same at another spot on the ring, space four or five of these bundle wrappings evenly round the disc.

5 When you have done this, cut off the remaining contrasting colour bundle and start a new bundle of the original body colour. Wrap this round so that it covers up the spaced out bundles completely. Carry on with this colour until no more wool will pass through the middle of the disc.

6 Using strong scissors, push one blade of the scissors into the wool and between the two card discs and cut the wool round the rim.

fluffy ladybird

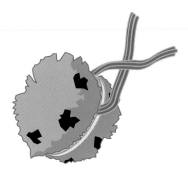

7 Pass several short strands of the wool between the discs and tie tightly round the bundle and cut off below the ends of the pompom. DO NOT remove the cardboard discs, for now just put the tied off pompom to one side while you make the body.

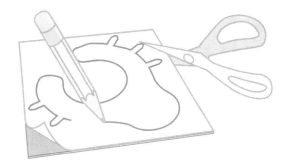

10 Trace the body template guides from the template page. Glue the guide to a thin piece of detergent bottle plastic and cut out carefully.

8 Spray or marker a small drink bottle cap black. Use an office hole punch to cut some thin card or detergent bottle plastic for the eyes, dot with a marker and glue in place. Apply a spot of glue-gun glue to the bottle cap and position eye on the end of a pin.

11 Spray or paint the body part black and stick the head in place.

9 Straighten two paper clips and poke through cap top and glue inside cap. Glue beads on the ends of the paper clips.

x 6

12 Cut six bendy drinking straws to about 45mm long so that the bendy bit is in the middle (use dark or black ones if you have them).

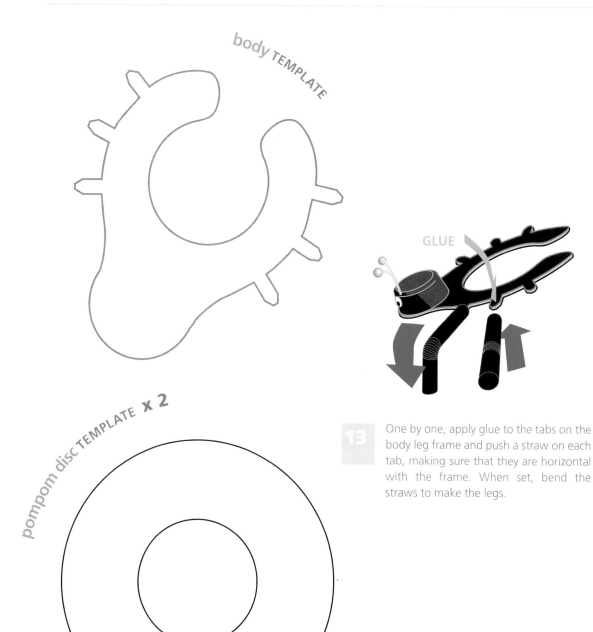

body TEMPLATE

pompom disc TEMPLATE **x 2**

GLUE

13 One by one, apply glue to the tabs on the body leg frame and push a straw on each tab, making sure that they are horizontal with the frame. When set, bend the straws to make the legs.

14 Now take your pompom body and cut or push only one of the discs off the bundle and slide the body leg assembly into the pompom middle, over the remaining disc. When legs are in place, cut or push the other disc off the pompom.

15 Further bend the legs round so that your ladybird stands straight. Trim the pompom back very hard, to get the right shape, especially underneath.

If a ladybird lands on you it's good luck, so make some luck for yourself with this fluffy pompom bug.

paper butterfly

A lovely little project that's just like a magic trick

8 years +

15 minutes

Wrapping paper
Strong thread

Make this beautiful butterfly in about five minutes using just a small scrap of old wrapping paper. This project is perfect if you are making your own greetings cards or simply want to decorate your room with something pretty.

When you've finished making the wings and have spread them out, you can customise your butterfly as much as you want. Make it out of brown paper and tie it off with parcel string to make a moth, or design a special butterfly all of your own by using plain paper and colouring it in with felt pens. You could also tie a small piece of pipe cleaner round the middle on the body to make the head, abdomen and thorax of the butterfly, blob glue-gun glue on the body and colour it with marker, or stick beads or sequins to create beautifully iridescent butterfly scales.

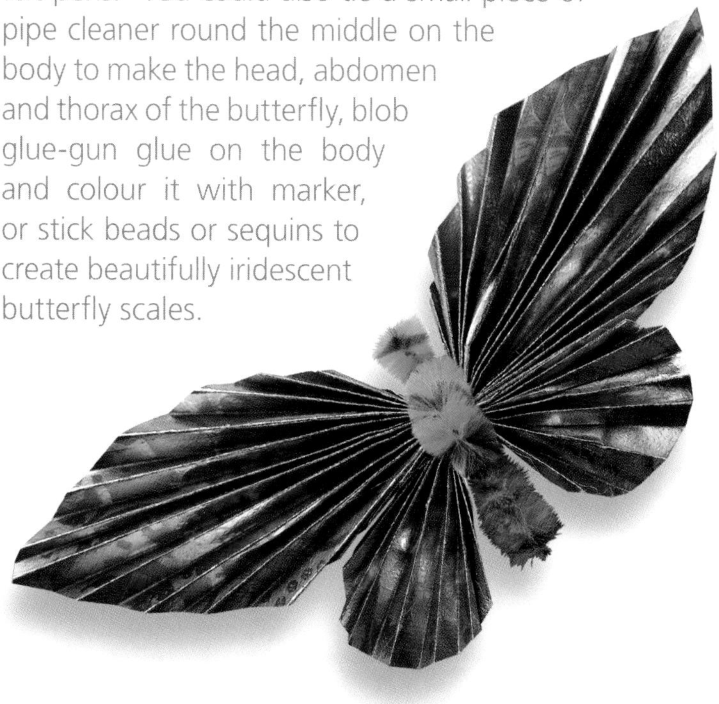

1 On any scrap piece of nice bright wrapping paper, draw a square about 90mm x 90mm, and a circle using the top of a glass or cup as a guide.

4 Continue to pleat the flap back and forth making sure you keep it neat and in straight lines. This is not as easy as it looks, but it gets easier as you practise.

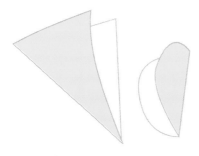

2 Carefully cut out the square and the circle and fold them both neatly in half.

5 Continue pleating until there is nothing more to fold, then turn the paper over and pleat up the other side. This is easier if you hold it in your hand rather than rest it on the table to fold it. Do the same with the circle.

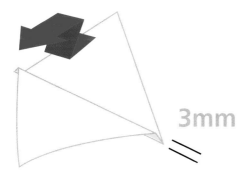

3 Begin to pleat one side of the square with thin pleats. To pleat, fold the flap back on itself and then back the other way.

6 When both the square and circle are pleated, pinch them together, between thumb and forefinger, tightly in the middle.

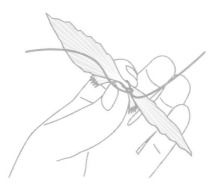

7 Holding both pleated pieces together, tie some thread around their middle and tie it tightly in a knot. You'll need someone to help you do this.

9 ... you can add a bit of pipe cleaner stuck on with white glue or glue-gun glue to make the butterfly's body.

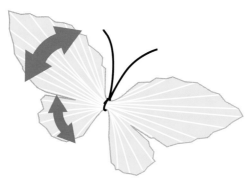

8 Fan out the square and the circle on both sides of the tie to make the four wings, and that's it. You can use the tie as the butterfly's antennae or...

Use a wire coathanger and some thread to create a beautiful butterfly mobile.

fish doorhandles

As Forrest Gump said, "It's funny what a young man recollects". Like him, I don't remember being born, nor what I got for my first birthday, but I do remember the pattern on the curtains in my first bedroom – African animals running across an ochre linen landscape as the fabric fluttered in the gentle breeze.

It's the unique little details on handmade things that make them into something that we become attached to, and that help turn our houses into homes. Bright colours, stencil painting or funky handles can transform even the most boring piece of furniture into a flight of fancy.

These simple fish handles make an exciting, mesmerising and memorable accessory and will bring any kid's room to life.

Brighten up a bedroom and inspire your kids

12 years +

3 hours

Jigsaw
Drill
Small piece of wood
   or MDF sheet
Threaded screw with
   nut
Small section of
   metal tubing
Newspaper
Wood glue
Glue gun
Paint

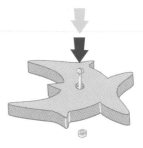

1 Trace the template and stick it to a small piece of thin plywood or MDF sheet about 10mm thick, and carefully cut out both fish shapes using a jigsaw. For simplicity, the instructions only show the big fish being made, however, follow each step for the small fish as well.

3 Push a long, thin, threaded bolt (about 60mm, M4) through the hole so that the bolt head is flush with the top of the wood. Fill over the bolt head with glue so that the bolt is firmly fixed in place.

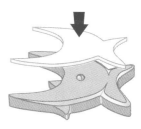

4 Carve, file or sandpaper the edges of the wooden shape to soften the top of the fish. To save time building up the shape, stick a slightly smaller cardboard fish shape to the top face of the fish. For the best effect, the tongue and the fins should be thinner than the body.

2 Drill a stepped hole in the centre of each fish. Drill the large hole first (only halfway through the wood), then drill the small hole. Be careful not to drill into the table or bench you are resting the work on. It's best to use an old bit of wood underneath to support your work piece and protect your table.

5 Add additional details using repeated applications of glue-gun glue. This will speed up the project and reduce the number of papier-mâché layers needed to get a nicely shaped fish. The fish does not need to be shaped on the back.

fish doorhandles

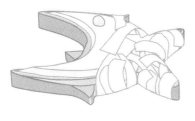

6 Cover the fish in papier-mâché strips. Use thin strips of newspaper dipped in watered down white woodwork glue (PVA). Water down using two parts glue to one part water. Cover the entire fish, smoothing out or building up features as desired.

little fish TEMPLATE

big fish TEMPLATE

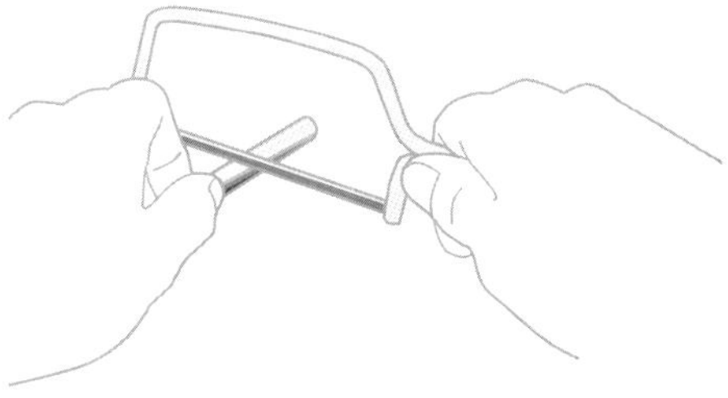

7 Allow the fish to dry out completely before painting. While it is drying, cut two short lengths of tubing to use as spacers for the bolt fixings, so that the handles will stand proud of the door. Metal curtain rod is ideal, but any narrow tube will do; you could even use a felt pen or ballpoint pen barrel.

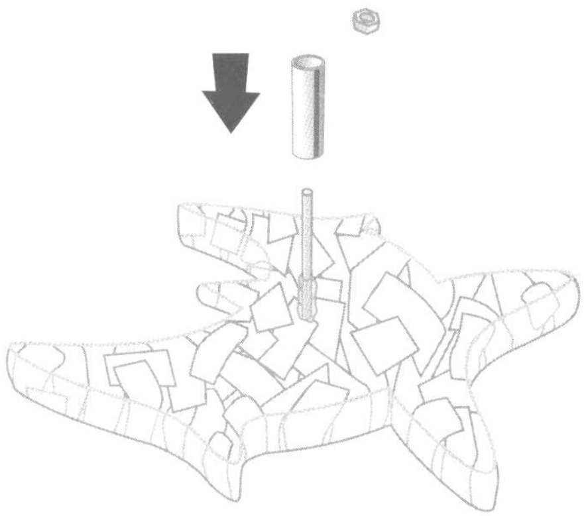

8 When the papier-mâché is completely dry, usually overnight or at least after a few hours in an airing cupboard, paint it white with water-based house emulsion. Then, when that is dry, put a blob of glue round the base of the bolt and glue the spacer tube into place.

9 Paint and varnish your fish. Choose bright exciting colours – look on the web for pictures of tropical fish, or even make up some fantastic designs of your own. Finally drill a small hole in your cupboard door and fit the new handles. Use a small washer under the nut if necessary to stop the nut pulling through the door wood.

TIP: The handles overlap slightly, so arrange them so that the little one doesn't extend on to the opposite door and close that one first.

Experiments in the kitchen are really good fun. This one shows which dyes are used to make the colours in children's felt pens, and as well as being quick and enjoyable it's also highly scientific. The experiment can be used as a basis for some interesting discussions about colour and the fact that even dye molecules have different weights (mass, if

you want to get technical). It will reinforce things your kids will be learning at school at some point, and the resulting strips can be dried out and kept in the special booklet that you can print out from our website.

Keep any discussion about the experiment brief and to the point so that they don't lose interest. On p51 you'll find an experimental discussion outline with a few key interesting facts. This is designed to help you fire up your children's interest, and to explain simply what's going on in the experiment if they ask.

Find out what dyes are used in your felt pens

I don't believe in dumbing things down for children, they are learning machines hungry for interesting bits of information. As long as you use words that they understand, you'll find that kids of any age readily grasp new concepts. Discuss the experiment with them as you are doing it. At the same time, make sure you listen to what they are saying, because when they are relaxed and having fun the things they talk about are a good window on how they are thinking and feeling.

6 years +

20 minutes

Blotting paper or
    coffee filter paper
Scissors
Wire coathanger
Plastic packaging

download available

Cut some strips of blotting paper or white coffee filter paper about 10mm x 150mm. Fold about 15mm.

Cut the long piece wire coathanger ar into a stand like th

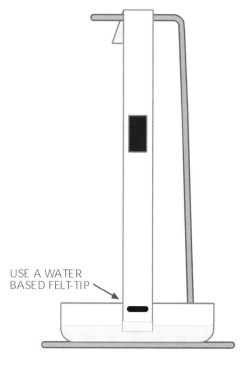

USE A WATER BASED FELT-TIP

Mark, then trim the bottom off a plastic packaging container (eg, a spread pack), to make water reservoir, about 15mm high.

Fill the reservoir with water to a depth of about 5mm.

Draw a single short horizontal line of the desired colour 10mm from the bottom of the blotting paper strip.

Hang strip on stand and that it is hang free the bottor about 2–3n the botton reservoir.

Colour a small square of the same colour on a piece of normal paper, cut out, and stick to the strip about two thirds of the way up.

Hang the strip on the stand so its end dips in the water, making sure the felt pen line is above the water level.

9 When colours are separated out, remove strip and lay on another piece of blotting paper to dry.

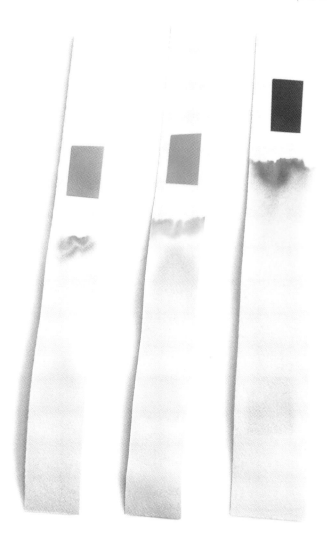

What makes the water go up the blotting paper?

The attraction of the water to the blotting paper molecules is stronger than the forces holding the water molecules to each other (this is called capillary action).

Why does the ink separate out?

The different dyes used to make up the felt-tip colours are made of molecules of different weights and the water can carry the less heavy dye molecules further up.

What are the primary colours?

Red, blue and yellow. These are colours that can't be mixed using other colours. Any two of the primary colours mixed together makes a secondary colour. These are the reflective primary colours. The primary colours of light (transmissive colours) are red, green and blue (RGB).

How is chromatography used in the real world?

Scientists use a range of solvents (like the water that you used), to find out which molecules are in chemicals. DNA is separated out using a similar process of molecular dye markers in a gel.

When it really matters

These tips are good advice for any father, but they are the Ten Commandments for newly separated and single dads. There is no more crucial time in a child's life for them to know that they can rely on you, than after you and their mother have separated. When a child's parents separate it blows their whole world apart. Their home is different, they see their parents crying every day, and even happy times can carry the threat of upset. There is no quick way out of this situation for your children, but you can make it less bad by being there for them. Read these ten tips and take them seriously. If you are able to follow them you will be doing some of the best and most considerate things you will ever do for your children.

Even with the best will in the world, when times are tough you will make mistakes, no one can get it right all the time. So when you go wrong, just mentally go back to this list and try harder next time to be there for your kids when they need you most.

1 Be reliable

When you go to get or meet your kids, always be on time. Make every effort to do what you say you're going to do and don't make promises you can't keep. If you agree to pick them up from school or go to a school event, write the date down when you are agreeing it. It's very easy to forget the exact details and end up letting your kids down.

2 Be a grown-up

Remember that you are the adult here. You will be dealing with a huge amount of emotion and hurt, but your children will be in pain too, and they shouldn't have to worry about looking after you. It's your job to care for them.

3 Build and keep to a routine

Keep to a routine, even if that means making a new one up. Periods of change are very unsettling for children, so even doing a simple activity at the same time, every time you see them, will become something they can rely on. This could be something as straightforward as getting a bun each from the same shop on the way to your house, or always having the same favourite meal on a certain night.

4 Listen to your kids

The little things your children say and do will give you a good idea about how they are feeling. Often feelings of anxiety will come out as a change in the way a child does things, the things that they say, or minor upsets like headaches or tummy aches. Try to think outside the immediate problem and look at the bigger view. Most importantly, listen. It's all too easy to forget to listen to your children when you are preoccupied with your own problems.

5 Support your kids' mother

Never tell your children that their mother is bad, or make nasty, snide or cynical comments about her to them. They love their mother unconditionally because she is their mother, just as they love you unconditionally because you are their father. However much you may feel wronged by your ex-partner, or partner, your children don't need to know right now.

In the long run putting their mother down to or in front of your children will backfire on you, because as they grow up they will come to see the situation for what it is. They won't thank you for trying to score points off their mother when they were vulnerable. Where possible, however hard it may seem, try to support their mother. If you have issues with her, discuss them and work together to make sure she supports you too.

6. Make your house or flat a real home

Ensure that your home is a special place for your kids to stay. Think of things and ways of doing things that will establish your new flat or house as more than just a place to visit. Make it into their other home. See p253 for some useful tips and advice on how to do this.

7. Remember you are in it for the long game

Think of it like this – you might recently have had to rely on your mother or father, and how old are you? Your children don't just need you now, they will always need you, and the relationship you build with them is a very long-term one. This is something to remember when it all goes wrong one weekend, as it sometimes will. Being a father is about more than just one weekend; it's for life.

8. Put excitement in their lives

You're the best person for the job and as a big kid at heart, you're well equipped to do it. But excitement can be brought into children's lives in many ways, and it doesn't mean endless treats. It's hard not to overcompensate for the fact that you are seeing them less, but

hold back. Think about it – it's not a treat for them to come and see you, any more than it's a treat that they see their mother the rest of the time. So try and put that to one side and think of the smaller ways to add light to their lives. This could be with something as simple as a new toothbrush, or putting a weird topping on a pancake you just made together.

9. Never quiz your kids

However curious or desperate you are to know what is going on at their other home, never try to find out information about your ex-partner from your children. Resist the temptation to use your kids for sending messages to their mother, and resist fishing for information. Your children didn't ask to be caught up in this and they are very sensitive to the fact that they have to go between their mum and dad, so the last thing you want them to feel when they're with you is that is that they have to be on their guard. If you are unable to communicate with your ex-partner directly, use another adult, preferably a mutual friend or grown-up family member, to pass important messages.

Never discuss contentious issues on the doorstep when you come to pick the children up or drop them off. If a disagreement starts on more than one occasion the children may begin to feel anxious about the handover, or start to dread you coming to pick them up or Mummy dropping them off.

10. Support your kids

To understand your children better, engage the child in you. If you don't already know, you'll find that you can communicate with your kids in ways their mother will never be able to.

space rocket PAGE 164

You know – fathers just have a way of putting everything together.

ERIKA COSBY
Daughter of Bill Cosby, US actor/singer

jeans pencil roll

Encourage the artist in your kids by making this really useful pencil roll together

12 years +

1 hour

Rectangle of fabric
Glue gun
Pencil

If you've got an old pair of jeans that you no longer wear, don't throw them away – make them into something. A pencil roll is a must for any budding artist, and is just what you need to keep all your best sketching pencils neatly in order and in perfect condition.

We've made our pencil roll from old denim, (there's something so cool about that) but of course, any old trousers, curtains, canvas, upholstery or other reasonably robust fabric will work just as well. We've used a glue gun to make the whole thing, which means you don't need a sewing machine. However, if you have a sewing machine, just replace the glue gun instruction steps with sewing machine ones and you'll get an excellent result.

jeans pencil roll

1 Cut a square of fabric from the leg of some old jeans, use the full circumference of the leg and a height of about 360mm. You can use any thick canvas-like fabric.

For this project we will be using a glue gun for all the seams, but you can just as easily use a sewing machine if you have one, or other fabric glue.

2 Fold over a small edge seam round each edge of about 5-10mm and glue in place all round.

3 Using either a pencil or ballpoint pen, on the inside of the material, mark some guidelines as shown. Start by drawing the horizontal lines at 90mm and then 80mm and 40mm, then draw the vertical lines about 30mm apart.

4 Put thin neat vertical strips of glue between the bottom two horizontal lines over the vertical lines you have marked. Work quickly to avoid the glue setting and only glue half the lines before carefully folding over the bottom flap to cover them.

5 When the first bit of glue has set gently peel back the free, unglued part and continue applying glue to the other vertical marks before folding the bottom flap up again and glueing completely in place.

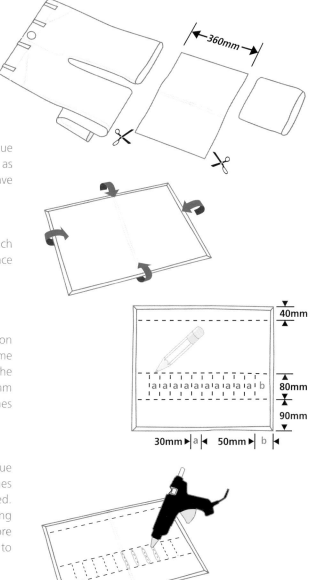

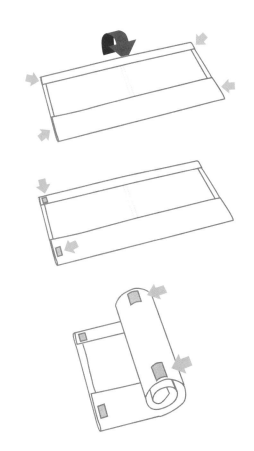

6   Put a thin strip of glue down each corner edge and glue the bottom edges neatly together and then fold over the smaller top flap and glue along the edge at each end.

7   Use a glue gun to glue a small rectangle of hook and eye fastener at the extreme edge of the top and bottom flaps (as shown).

8   To make sure that the other part of the hook and eye fastener is in the right place, loosely roll up the pencil roll (or roll up tightly with pencils in) and mark where the other part of the fastener should go. Then glue in exactly the right place.

Displays your pencils in a really handy way and also protects them from getting broken.

doughnut

Make this delicious-looking treat, just like the doughnuts Homer Simpson loves so much, in under a hour. All you'll need are two lightweight carrier bags, some sticky tape and a bit of glue-gun glue. Prepare to step into the world of modern, no-wait papier-mâché!

This is papier-mâché with a difference. Instead of bits of paper you are going to use old carrier bags to give your model bulk and form, and instead of wet glue, you are going to use masking tape, so you won't have to wait for ages for it to dry. This is really a very easy model to make, and it will show you how you can use glue-gun glue to do a form of rudimentary modelling. Be careful when using the glue gun and read the 'Before you start' section on p16 for tips on safe use.

A plastic-bag doughnut that looks good enough to eat!

12 years +

1 hour

Masking tape
Glue gun
Spray paint
Sugar strands

doughnut

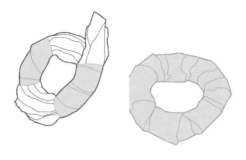

1 Curl one lightweight plastic carrier bag round into a doughnut shape and wrap in masking (or normal sticky) tape.

2 Take a second bag, tear in half lengthways and wrap round doughnut until it looks about the right thickness.

3 Wrap the doughnut in masking tape so that it is as smooth as possible.

4 Coat the top of the doughnut in a liberal layer of glue-gun glue so that some dribbles down the side.

5 Do one half at a time, but coat the second half while the first is still hot so that the edges merge. Don't put too much on otherwise it will run everywhere. **Note: glue-gun glue is hot and will burn if it gets on you.**

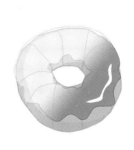

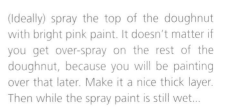

6 (Ideally) spray the top of the doughnut with bright pink paint. It doesn't matter if you get over-spray on the rest of the doughnut, because you will be painting over that later. Make it a nice thick layer. Then while the spray paint is still wet...

doughnut

7 Sprinkle sugar strands over the top of the doughnut so that they stick in the wet paint. If you don't have spray paint then you can get this effect by painting white glue (PVA, that dries clear) over your pink paint and sprinkling the sugar strands on to that while it is wet.

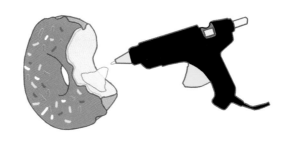

10 To make the filling, build up a big blob of glue-gun glue.

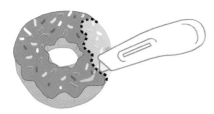

8 Cut through glue-gun glue with a strong craft knife and then cut the tape and plastic bag doughnut with a pair of scissors or long thin knife in a sawing action. If you don't want a bite then skip to step 14.

11 The blob will want to sag or drip, so keep turning doughnut as it sets (see next two steps).

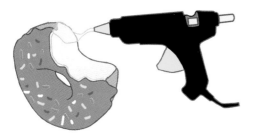

9 Seal the cut face with a thin layer of glue-gun glue.

12 Build up the blob over two or three goes, a big blob of hot glue takes much longer to set and will be hard to control.

▶

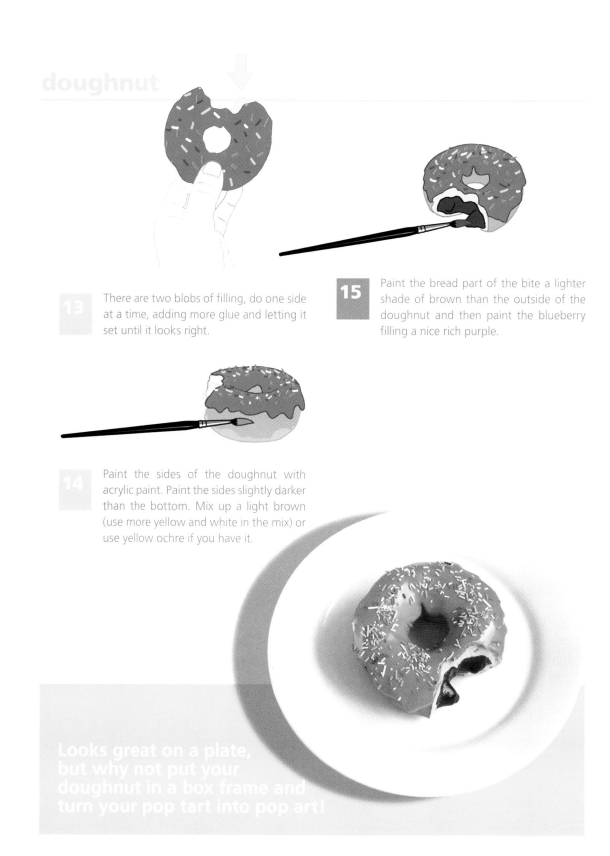

doughnut

13 There are two blobs of filling, do one side at a time, adding more glue and letting it set until it looks right.

15 Paint the bread part of the bite a lighter shade of brown than the outside of the doughnut and then paint the blueberry filling a nice rich purple.

14 Paint the sides of the doughnut with acrylic paint. Paint the sides slightly darker than the bottom. Mix up a light brown (use more yellow and white in the mix) or use yellow ochre if you have it.

Looks great on a plate, but why not put your doughnut in a box frame and turn your pop tart into pop art!

bookbinding

Now you can bind your own hardback book in the same way that bookbinders have been doing it for generations. All you need are some spare sheets of paper, old cardboard and almost any left over pieces of fabric or leather. Make a holiday book, personalised diary or a special birthday book, and to add a personal touch, simply print out a header and footer on the pages before you bind them. This project shows you the basics, but after you have made your first book, you might want to experiment with binding in different types of paper.

For the cover you can use almost any material: specially bought fabric, leather from an old coat or handbag, felt, curtains, old cushion covers. Josie, a dadcando website member, customised her denim book cover by glueing one of the jeans pockets on to the front of the book to keep her pens and pencils in.

A beautiful sheet of marbled lining paper is available to print out from our website.

A beautiful hardback book made and bound by you

12 years +

1 hour (incl. glue drying)

Paper
PVA glue
Cardboard
Fabric
Stapler
Coloured paper or marbled printable

download available

bookbinding

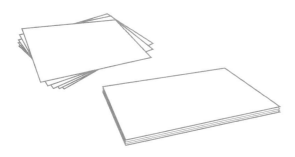

1 Take eight A4 sheets of paper and stack them neatly.

2 Fold the whole stack over as neatly as possible.

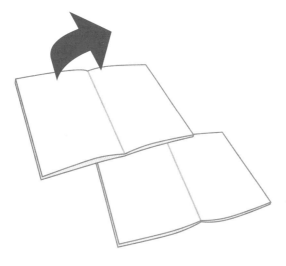

3 Unfold the stack. Turn the stack over and make sure that all the pages are still aligned.

4 If you don't have a long arm stapler, open up a normal office stapler.

5 Using a slow firm action press a staple out through the paper and into an eraser positioned under the paper.

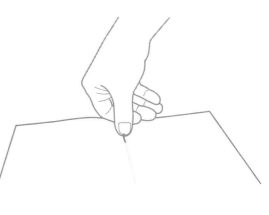

6 Staple both ends about 2cm in from the edge and turn over, then carefully fold over the open staples with your thumb or a suitable blunt edge. Ideally make four (or more) of these eight-sheet folios.

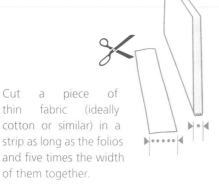

7 Cut a piece of thin fabric (ideally cotton or similar) in a strip as long as the folios and five times the width of them together.

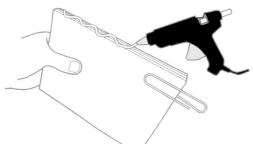

8 Holding the folios tightly together, glue the edges of the spines with glue-gun glue or PVA glue (only covering the edges).

11 Place the folios on some old stiff cardboard and draw round allowing a border of about 5mm.

9 Press the folios' spine on to the fabric taking care not to glue the fabric to the sides by mistake.

12 Cut out two of the same size book covers (cut one then trace round it for the second).

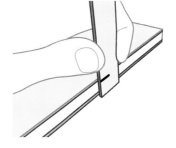

10 If you want you can now trim the folios so that they have a neat edge. This takes practice. Be very careful with the craft knife.

13 Assemble the covers and the folios and using a piece of scrap card, measure the depth of the combined covers and folios together.

▶

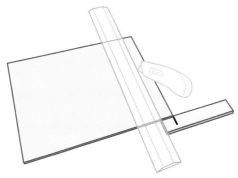

16 Glue the covers and spine in place using PVA (white glue) or Copydex spread evenly using a scrap of card as a spatula.

14 Using the depth marker cut a strip of cardboard for the spine, the same height as the cover pieces.

17 Glue the border over as neatly as possible taking care with the corners. For thicker fabrics you might have to cut off some of the hidden corner fold to avoid it being too bulky at the corners.

15 Lay out the covers and spine on a piece of fabric or leather so that they are all aligned and are spaced two thicknesses of card apart. Then mark the fabric with a border of about 25mm all round and neatly cut out to the mark.

18 Apply glue to, and spread evenly over, only the centre-most parts of the cover (NOT THE SPINE).

19 Glue the flaps from the spine binding fabric to the covers (DO NOT GLUE IT TO THE COVER SPINE).

22 Fold over your lining paper and glue one half at a time to the front page and to the inside of the front cover. Repeat for the back.

20 Print out the downloadable marbled paper, make your own or buy some and cut out.

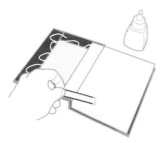

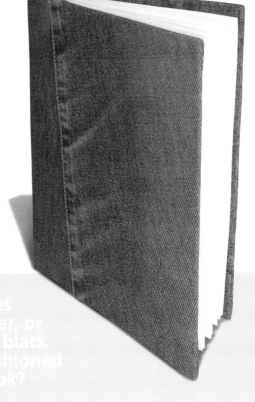

21 Neatly paste the first page and the inside of the cover with glue. Make the glue even and paste right up to the edge.

Why not bind in different types of paper, tissue or tracing paper, or perhaps dark, rich coloured or black paper, to make a lovely old fashioned photograph album or scrapbook?

painted egg

Learn the ancient art of egg blowing and then paint beautiful eggs like these

8 years +

45 minutes
(incl. glue drying)

1 x Hen's egg
Glue gun
Cocktail stick
Scissors
Paint (that dries
waterproof)

download available

There is something about the fragility of an egg, coupled with its small size and simplicity, which has always fascinated artists. Then there's the whole art of blowing an egg; an exciting experiment all of its own. However, once you start painting the blown egg, you quickly realise that the hardest part is actually holding the thing steady while painting it. This project shows you how to make a special little holder to make sure that you can easily paint your egg for the best results.

Using good, fluid, bright paints and a nice new thin brush will make the job much more satisfying. If you design your egg first, you can go out together to the craft or art shop and buy a few little tins of quick-drying enamel and a small brush as part of the activity.

1 Gently wash the egg in cold soapy water, and then rinse and dry.

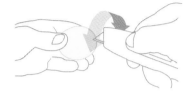

2 Carefully using the tip of a sharp craft knife, rotate back and forth on the same spot until you make a small hole at one end.

3 It can take up to five minutes to make a neat hole. Don't rush or force the blade, because then you will crack the egg. Do the same at both ends. Run a cocktail stick through the egg to pierce the inner membrane.

4 Gently hold the egg to your lips and blow the contents out. Rinse the inside of the egg under a tap and by blowing water through it.

5 Put some glue-gun glue on the end of a cocktail stick and glue the stick into the egg at one end. Hold steady till it is set.

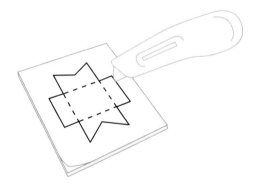

6 Trace the egg holder template on to a piece of thick card and carefully cut it out using scissors or a craft knife.

7 Fold up the egg holder and stick the corners using glue-gun glue or sticky tape.

▶

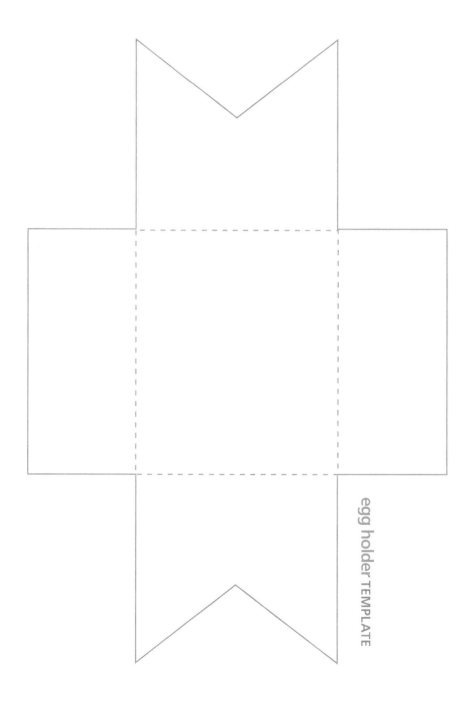

egg holder TEMPLATE

8 Design your egg pattern or visit our website to print out some design templates.

9 Spray or paint the egg a bright colour to start with, it gives you a head start and makes the egg look nice straight away.

10 Place the egg in the holder and paint your design. Rotate the egg using the tips of the cocktail stick, resting your hand on a book pushed up to the holder.

11 When your egg is dry, very carefully work the cocktail stick loose or cut it off with a pair of strong scissors.

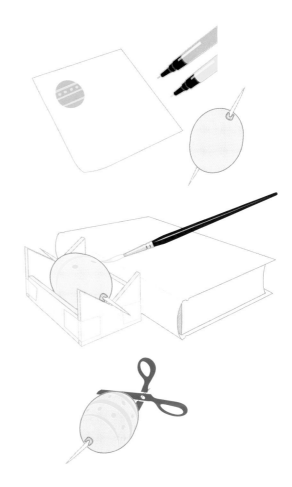

Display your egg in a nest, or turn the page to make your own egg stand.

egg stand

What better way to display your hand blown, painted eggs than with this delicate egg stand?

12 years +

1 hour
(incl. glue drying)

Paper
PVA glue
Cardboard
Fabric
Stapler
Coloured paper or
marbled printable

download available

You can use thick paper or medium weight card to make this great looking Egg Stand. Print out a coloured stand in ebony or cherry from our website or make your own in ivory, jade, silver or gold, using the outline templates provided. This is a really simple, good-looking project that will give you the perfect platform to show off your handpainted pieces.

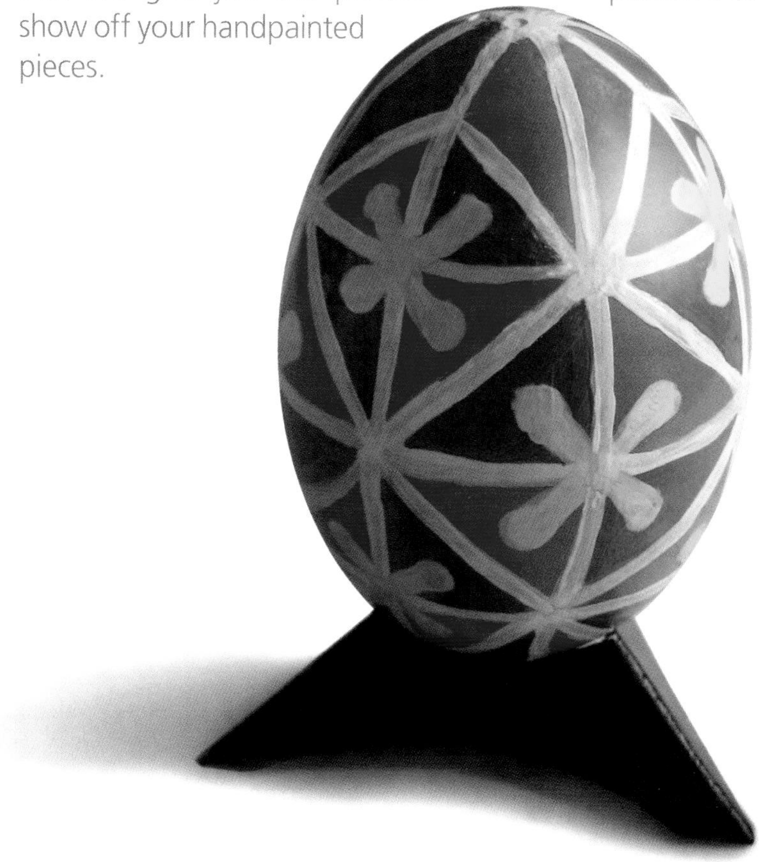

egg stand

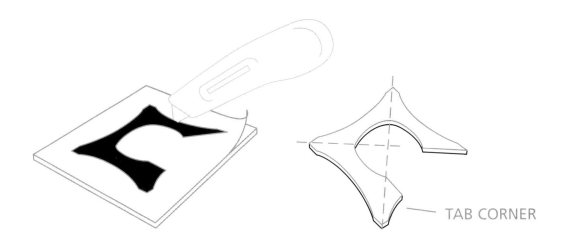

TAB CORNER

1 Trace the egg stand template on p74 on to a medium weight card or thick stiff paper if you have it. If not, trace on to normal paper and stick it to a piece of thin cardboard.

Carefully cut out using a craft knife or strong scissors.

3 Turn over the cut out and make a deep crease from corner to corner on the back on the three corners that have folds. That is, the two main corners and the one with the tab.

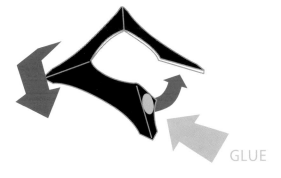

GLUE

2 Alternatively, use either the cherry or ebony printables, or use the blank outlines and colour your own stand to look like jade (green), ivory (very pale yellow), gold or silver. Carefully cut out using a craft knife or strong scissors.

4 Turn back over and fold the stand at the creases.

Put a blob of glue-gun glue or PVA on the tab, (this will take a while to dry and will need to be held while drying) or stick a small piece of double-sided sticky tape on to the tab.

▶

egg stand

egg stand 1 TEMPLATE

egg stand 2 TEMPLATE

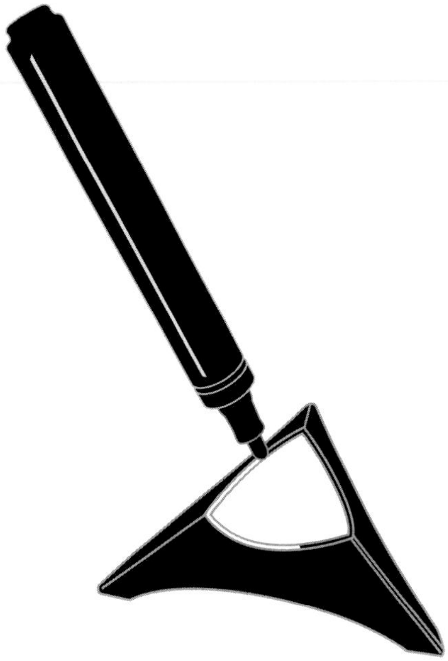

5 Glue the tab neatly to the inside of the free corner. Colour the cut cardboard edges in with a similar coloured marker.

Now your stand is ready to present your painted eggs.

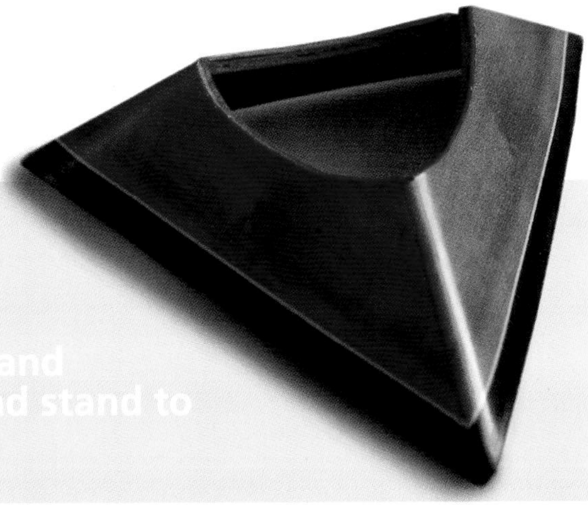

Make a Victorian glass dome and show off your painted egg and stand to perfection (see p236)

kokeshi doll

Kokeshi (小芥子), are simple Japanese dolls turned from wood that came from northern Japan in the 17th century. The beauty of this project is that you can make one in a few minutes or spend the whole afternoon on design, spraying and careful painting – the only limit is your imagination.

All you need for the head and hair are two old packaging lids of slightly different sizes. For the head, the lid needs to have a rounded top, which you will turn upside-down to make the curved visible bit of the face, with the bigger lid forming the hair. For the body you can use a simple product bottle cut down to size.

So try your hand at making a Kokeshi Doll, approach it with peace and create your very own lucky charm.

One of the most collectible toys in Japan – now you can make your own!

8 years +

30 minutes

Spray or deodorant roll-on caps
Bottles
Glue gun

kokeshi doll

1 Look for a small plastic bottle with simple curves. Hair products and mini yoghurt drinks are suitable. Also you will need two large aerosol or roll-on deodorant caps of slightly different sizes so that one fits over the other.

always mark before cutting

2 Search on the web for pictures of Kokeshi dolls that you would like to copy. Mark on the bottle and the product pack lids and cut out using strong scissors. The fringe should be low so that only a small bit of face is showing.

3 If you have very fine wet and dry emery paper (p600 or finer), rub down the plastic bottle, to provide a key for the paint, then paint or spray the bottle a nice bright colour. If you have more than one colour, fade between them.

4 Take the larger of the two caps and after rubbing down the surface with fine emery paper, spray or paint it a suitable dark colour. You can hold the piece on a slightly crushed cardboard toilet paper tube, pushed inside the cap.

5 Decorate the body of the doll using paints and permanent felt-tip pen markers. Look at traditional Kokeshi dolls on the web and try to learn about how the Kokeshi doll maker stylishly portrays a simple face, then copy it.

6 Glue the head to the top of the bottle and the hair over the head. Kokeshi dolls are simple and elegant. Practise this simple project until you are able to convey some of those unique and peaceful qualities in your dolls.

Check on the web for Kokeshi doll designs to inspire you, and think up more along the lines of ninjas, manga or sumo.

paint a shirt

Painting a T-shirt is really easy; it's the perfect way to spend the afternoon, and your kid will have something great to wear at the end of it. Fabric paint is not expensive and if you buy just a few colours you can mix a bit of acrylic paint with them to get the exact colour you want.

The key with any designing or making project is to have a good idea of what you want to do before you actually start making. All you have to do is start with something you like. Simplify it in your mind or on paper, so that you are not making your job too difficult – remember simpler is better. More often the images that look best on a T-shirt are the simple, striking ones, so get sketching right away. Any extra effort you put in at the beginning getting the design right will pay off in the finished article.

All you need to know to make a fun and original T-shirt

7 years +

90 minutes

Plain white T-shirt
Fabric paint
Paintbrush and
  marker
Clothes iron

paint a shirt

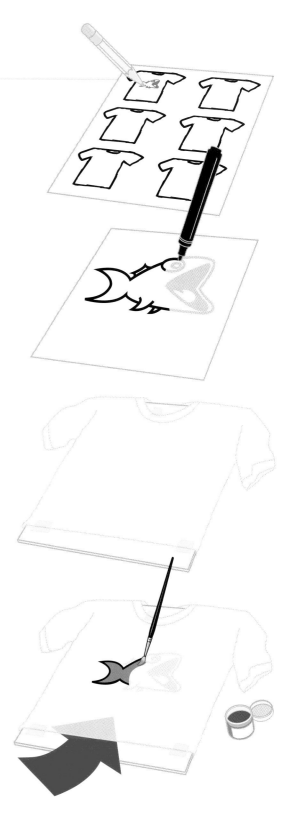

1 The most important part of any good project is the design. Start by designing your T-shirt on a sheet with some T-shirt shapes drawn on it. Use references from a book, a DVD or your favourite console game.

2 Once you have a design that you are happy with, enlarge it on to a separate piece of paper. You can enlarge it by eye or by photocopier. Use a thick black marker to draw the outline. Don't colour the picture in at this stage, because you need it to be as clear as possible, so that you can see it through the T-shirt fabric.

3 Next you will need to slightly stretch your T-shirt to provide a good surface to paint on. Put some flat cardboard, or an up-turned tea tray inside the T-shirt. To make sure that it doesn't move while you are painting, stick the shirt to the board with a few small pieces of sticky tape.

4 Slip the enlarged design under the fabric, on top of the board and position it exactly where you want it to be. Now carefully begin to paint the T-shirt, following the design that you can just see through the fabric. You will need a smallish brush with only a little bit of paint on it at a time. Be careful not to overload your brush, as the paint will bleed into the T-shirt fabric and make blobs on your design. Be very careful not to smudge your hand across the parts that you have already painted. Start with the light colours and paint the darker ones over the top of them. IMPORTANT: Fabric paint does not wash out of clothes, so make sure you are wearing old painting clothes or an apron – BEFORE you start!

paint a shirt

5 Once you have finished painting your design, leave the T-shirt to dry for about 15 mins. Then carefully remove the stretching board and the template image. Be careful not to drag them out, because they might still have wet paint on them, and this will mark the inside of the shirt, which could show through. Dry the shirt using a hairdryer if you have one and you want the shirt to be finished quickly, otherwise leave to dry for an hour or so in a warm place.

6 When the design is completely dry, turn the T-shirt inside out and place an old tea towel inside it. This is a precaution in case the paint isn't completely dry (which invariably it isn't). Then iron over the design with the iron on its hottest setting (fabric permitting) to fix the design. The hottest setting is fine for most natural fabrics (like cotton), but if you have used a manmade material, check the label to see what the maximum setting of the iron can be before starting. ALWAYS supervise children if they are using an iron. Turn right side out and wear your T-shirt with pride at every opportunity.

For a simpler option, inkjet out a web image or photo from your digital camera and use iron-on, transfer printing paper to make a permanent design.

micro cans

Make these cute mini tin cans for action figures and dolls

8 years +

15 minutes

Glue gun
Hacksaw
Craft knife
Old felt-pen lids
Tin foil

download available

This is a really simple model, quick to make and there are so many possibilities. These tiny micro cans are absolutely perfect for action figures, where the tins can be made into army rations, or for small dolls. You can use the label printouts provided on our website to get you started, but it's far better if you and your kids design labels of your own. To do this you'll need to draw the labels bigger, with normal felt pens and pencils, scan them in to your computer, reduce them to the right size and then print them out. Alternatively, you could reduce them in size on a photocopier.

It really is as easy as it looks, the instructions show you how to make sure that they are all the same size. This project should take you about 10 minutes per can, less if you really get good at making them.

1. Take any old felt-pen lid, the best ones for the templates are 10mm to 11mm in diameter. The colour doesn't matter as it will all be covered up with straight sides.

4. Put a blob of glue-gun glue in one end of the sawn-off lid, being careful not to get any on the outside of the lid.

2. Carefully cut out a piece of paper 26 x 135mm and stick round the lid using sticky tape.

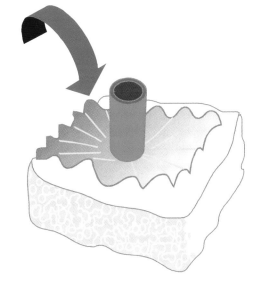

3. Using the edge of the paper as a guide, saw the lid crosswise with a metal hacksaw (this is a great safe way for kids to practise sawing).

5. Turn over the lid and press it down hard on to a small scrap of baking foil resting on a washing up sponge, so that it dents in.

▶

7 Trim the waste foil away so that the end and some of the sides are covered.

6 When the foiled end has cooled slightly, put a blob of glue-gun glue in the open end, turn over and repeat with another scrap of foil.

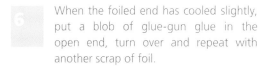

8 Carefully cut out one of the label templates, or make your own label, and wrap round the foil ended lid so that the same amount of lid sticks out of each end. Stick with double-sided tape, or use clear sticky tape.

Get creative and make spilled cans or open cans with their lids still attached.

micro books

Long car journeys between Mum's and Dad's, special weekends away; kids of separated parents often have to do a lot of travelling, and have a lot to keep in their heads. So, what better than a pocket-sized notebook to write and sketch down all those important thoughts? These fun little origami micro books are a really simple project that anyone can tackle. They're perfect for kids as they're small enough to fit in a pocket or a small bag and they don't have loads of pages that will never get written in. My kids showed me how to make a micro book in about five minutes, it's that quick and easy. See our website for graphic printables including holiday diaries that are perfect for keeping happy memories of a lovely time with Dad.

Catch all those important thoughts in this neat little notebook

7 years +

5 minutes

Sheet of A4 paper

download available

1. Place paper printed side down on a flat surface.

2. Fold in half lengthways, making sure that you fold carefully to make a straight, neat fold.

3. Unfold.

4. Now fold in half crossways, again making sure that you fold carefully to make a straight fold.

5. Fold in half crossways again. This is a bit harder because you are folding two thicknesses of paper, but still make sure you are accurate.

6. Now unfold the last fold you just made.

7. Carefully cut along the middle fold only halfway across the folded paper as shown.

8. Now, unfold the piece of paper completely so that it is A4 size again.

9. Still with printed side down, fold in half lengthways.

10. Rotate the whole piece so that it can stand on the table, or so that you can hold it upright.

micro books

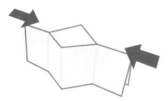

GLUE   GLUE

11 Gripping both ends between the thumbs and forefingers of both hands, push ends together.

13 If you want to make a really neat job of it, you can add a small dab of glue just inside both of the open corners (a glue stick is fine for this purpose).

12 Push ends together until you make a cross shape as shown, then fold the pages round to one side to make your book, making sure the front one is on the outside.

14 Rub the spine carefully with the back of a fingernail to make sure the booklet keeps its shape and stays closed.

Use a blank micro book to write and illustrate your first mini novel.

BIG KITCHEN SCIENCE

Turn your kitchen into a molecular factory

8 years +

2 hours

Deodorant balls
Cocktail sticks
Drinking straws

Atoms are the building blocks of all matter, and when they are found on their own, they are called elements. An atom is made up of a positively charged nucleus (itself made of protons) surrounded by negatively charged particles called electrons.

Carbon dioxide is made up of one carbon atom joined to two oxygen atoms. Plants respire using carbon dioxide, and use it in the presence of sunlight to make energy in a process called photosynthesis. The by-product is oxygen, useful for us and all the other animals on earth that need oxygen to live. Methane is a smelly gas made up of one carbon atom and four hydrogen atoms.

Water is the most common molecular compound on earth and is fundamental to life. Freezing at 0°C and boiling at 100°C, it covers almost 70 per cent of the earth's surface. It is nature's most powerful solvent, dissolving most things to some degree. It's strange to think of that clear liquid being made up of two highly reactive, invisible gases, but it is – water consists of one oxygen joined to two hydrogen atoms. To build your molecular models you will need some roll-on deodorant balls. You won't need many because you can reuse them in loads of different arrangements.

Deodorant roll-on balls are great for molecule making.

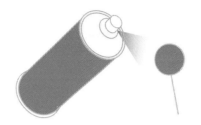

To remove the ball safely poke the tip of a pair of small scissors between the pack and the ball and cut three or four slits in the soft pack plastic and pop the roller ball out.

Holding the ball on a spare piece of cocktail stick or coathanger wire, spray or paint a nice bright colour.

Either wait and collect the deodorant balls, or just buy the cheapest deodorant and pour the deodorant away, or save in another container to refill other packs later.

Cut some equal size lengths of drinking straw (or any lightweight tubing) using a pair of scissors.

30mm

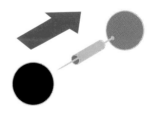

Mark the balls with small dots where you are going to drill. Look on the web to find what different molecules look like and how their bonds are traditionally shown. Start simple.

Push stick into hole and thread piece of straw followed by another ball. Use glue if you want a permanent structure.

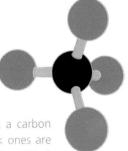

Drill a very small hole through the ball surface. Use a drill that is a tight fit for a cocktail stick or piece of wire coathanger.

9 If the black ball is a carbon atom and the pink ones are hydrogen atoms, then this is methane – smelly!

Who is credited with coming up with the stick and ball molecular model?

Niels Bohr, a Danish scientist (1885 – 1962).

How big is an atom?

Very small, about one ten millionth of a millimetre in diameter.

What is an element?

An element is the most basic type of matter which is composed of only one type of atom. Hydrogen (H), oxygen (O), carbon (C) and iron (Fe) are examples of elements.

What is a molecule?

A molecule is a compound made up when two or more atoms join together. Water (H_2O), carbon dioxide (CO_2), methane (CH_4) and common salt (sodium chloride, NaCl) are typical molecular compounds.

BEING THERE

Be prepared

The moments you have with your children are precious. Depending how much you see your kids, it is likely that both you and your child or children will be excited to see each other. Paradoxically this can end up being stressful, as you'll both put a lot of stock in this valuable time. Overexcitement can lead to headaches and other minor upsets, which are all physical ways of expressing the emotional stresses and strains of seeing someone you love when you haven't seen them for a while. If you are not prepared for this situation then you can waste time trying to get stuff at the last minute or have a spoiled weekend.

If, despite all the best preparation, things start to go wrong, take a deep breath and don't panic. If it's just a minor upset, then don't let it get to you, remember you are in this for the long game, and there'll be another weekend soon. If it's something major seek help from a neighbour or friend early on.

Some of these tips might seem a bit simple, but for me they have been about the most useful things that I have done to be prepared.

1. Keep some simple emergency medicines in your home

Be prepared to manage minor illnesses. There is nothing worse than a child becoming poorly during the night when you can't go out, or the shops are shut. Pick these items up the next time you are at the shops. There's no need to buy branded medicines, supermarket brands are much cheaper and just as good. To be prepared for the most common, rapid onset, minor children's complaints, such as mild headaches, toothache, tummy upsets, cuts and grazes, or a slight fever, you will need:

- 1 bottle children's paracetamol syrup
- 1 bottle children's ibuprofen syrup
- 1 bottle milk of magnesia
- 1 tube of antiseptic cream
- 1 packet of assorted size sticking plasters

Important notes and tips on medicines for children that visit or stay with Dad:

- Always read the label before giving medicines to a child.
- Make sure that your child isn't allergic to the medicine or any of its ingredients.
- Never give a child more paracetamol than the recommended dose
- Ibuprofen and paracetamol may be taken at the same time.
- If you are worried about the health of your child look online for help, talk to a pharmacist for advice, or contact your doctor.

If your child is taking a course of medicine such as antibiotics when they come to visit, make sure you understand the regime and follow it exactly. Take notes if necessary. Failing to finish a course of medicine at the very least will considerably reduce its efficacy and can seriously harm your child.

If your child comes to stay with you while ill and has been given any over-the-counter medicines like ibuprofen or paracetamol that day, find out when the last dose was given. Painkillers are dangerous if given more frequently than every four hours, so when a child is moving from one parent to the other it is important to establish these details. If you are bringing your child back, and you have given them any medicines while they have been at your house, tell their mother, or the adult into whose care you are passing the child, exactly what you have given them and when. Write it down for them so that it won't be confused later. Do not rely on your child to 'tell Mummy', children get this sort of thing mixed up and have a different perception of time.

Keep some simple emergency medicines in your car

Kids of parents who have separated often spend a significant amount of time in the car travelling between homes and then on to see grandparents and extended family. Be prepared to manage minor illness and headaches wherever you are. Having a few things handy can save the day on that special outing. The car is an easy thing to stock up. Buy wet wipes, some plastic cutlery and a roll of toilet tissue, put them in a carrier bag and keep them in the boot. Buy some antiseptic cream and plasters as in the previous list, a packet each of children's paracetamol and ibuprofen syrup sachets and some children's chewable antacid tablets.

Get a set of coloured felt pens, small paper scissors and sticky tape

Kids love colouring and drawing, and whether just sitting at home or going somewhere by car or train, having colouring pens and plain paper handy for them to use is a lifesaver. You don't have to get expensive felt pens, but washable ones and bright colours are a must. Check them regularly or watch while your children use them, and when they start running out, replace them. They're not expensive, and most supermarkets sell them. Remember how you used to love new felt pens when you were a kid, and how boring it was when every pen you picked up was on the way out?

Keep a stock of UHT milk

My children call it Emergency Milk. They don't really like it, because they're used to fresh pasteurised milk, but on the occasion that we run out and the shops are closed, Emergency Milk for cereal does come in handy.

Freeze sliced bread

When you are living on your own, food like bread can easily become stale before you have had a chance to eat it. If you freeze sliced bread, it keeps indefinitely. You can toast frozen bread straight from the freezer and make great packed lunch or picnic sandwiches from it while it is still frozen. When you've made your sandwiches, wrap them immediately in cling film and then in 10 minutes or less the bread will be defrosted and lovely and fresh.

If you wrap the sandwiches and put them in your insulated lunch box, they help keep the rest of the food cool.

6 Take small bottles of tap water with you when you go out

Kids get thirsty and you should always make sure that they have enough water to drink, especially on hot days, so save a few single-dose bottles, fill them with tap water and take them with you. This will save you filling up on canned fizzy drinks and it's loads cheaper. Keep a full one in the car.

7 Buy a simple tool and mending kit

It's not the sort of thing you pack up as you go to move out of your home, but in your new flat or house a small tool and mending kit will be very useful. Superglue and two-part resin are perfect for mending broken toys, and so are useful things for a dad to have around. Children should never be allowed to use superglue, though. Ideally you will need:

- A small screwdriver set
- A small torch
- A pair of strong kitchen scissors
- A roll of sticky tape
- 1 tube cyanoacrylate glue (superglue)
- 1 pair of tubes of two-part resin glue.

8 Freeze single-serving juice cartons

Great for packed lunches and picnics; the frozen drink slowly defrosts in the cooler bag, keeping everything nice and cool, and then by lunchtime it will be ready to drink but still nice and cold.

9 Buy some small Tupperware boxes so that you can freeze extra food you cook

When you cook for your kids, always make more than you need and freeze the spare. Use either cheap Tupperware boxes or any small plastic packaging pots, these are ideal for freezing the extra food in single serving portions and perfect for you to microwave another day, when you don't feel like cooking.

10 Buy a basic making kit

This book is about how you can do things with your kids. One of the most rewarding things you can do, for both you and your kids, is to make stuff with them. You don't need any equipment to start because some of the projects only require a piece of paper (fold-up shirts, for example), but for about £20 you can set yourself up with some basic equipment that will enable you to make the most fantastic toys and models from just about any old junk that you would normally throw away.

feather quill PAGE 146 magical ink pot PAGE 150

When I was a boy of fourteen, my father was so ignorant I could hardly stand to have the old man around. But when I got to be twenty-one, I was astonished at how much the old man had learned in seven years.

MARK TWAIN
Character of Samuel Clemens, author

WAVES AND WHEELS

helicopter PAGE 105

formula one racing car PAGE 101

EGG TIMER

being there
RELIABLE ROUTINES

122

steam train PAGE 112

floating container ship

Bathtime means perfect conditions for this ship's journey

One of the quickest models to put together, this floating container ship is made from a couple of old dishwasher or washing machine liquid bottles and a few other bits and pieces. It's not even sprayed, but plenty of fun was had making and playing with it. When it was made, my kids loved naming it in permanent marker, and then sailing it across the great Bath Ocean.

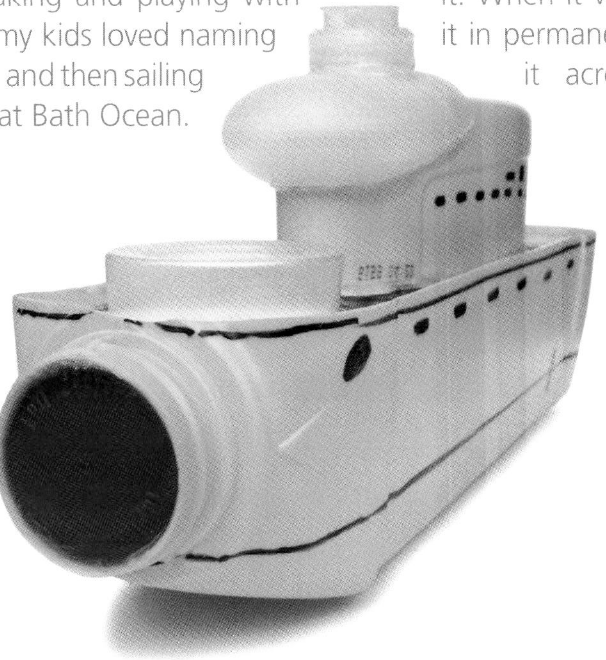

8 years +

40 minutes

Glue gun
Marker
Craft knife
Large dishwasher powder bottle
Small dishwasher powder bottle
Piece of cardboard
Shower gel bottle
2l milk carton cap
Washing-up liquid bottle cap
Yoghurt pot base

floating container ship

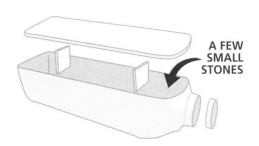

A FEW SMALL STONES

1 To make a floating ship you'll need a plastic bottle for the hull. Use a detergent bottle. Mark a line round the bottle using a permanent marker. Cut the hull from a large bottle, and the cabin from a smaller bottle.

4 Cut some small supports at the right height to allow the deck to be slightly recessed. Glue these to the underside of the deck. Glue round the edge of the deck and slide in. Glue the milk bottle top into detergent bottle opening. To stop your ship being top heavy, glue a few small stones inside the hull before you glue the deck into position.

GLUE

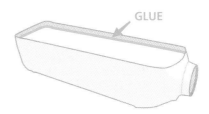

2 Place hull part upside down on a piece of thick card and draw round with a marker.

5 With deck in place glue round it to make sure it's waterproof.

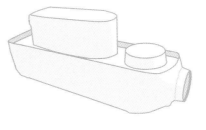

3 Cut out deck slightly inside the line so that the card will just fit inside the hull.

6 Glue the cabin upside down to the deck, then glue the yoghurt pot end to the deck.

▶

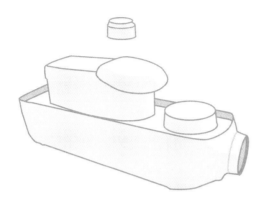

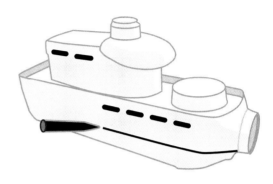

7 Cut the end off a shower gel pack and glue to the front of the cabin to make the bridge. Glue a washing up bottle top to the top of the bridge to make a funnel.

8 Decorate with marker, then play with it in the bath!

TIP: Let your children name the ship and launch it down the slope at the end of the bath.

floating submarine

One evening as bathtime approached there was a distinct lack of new and exciting bath toys. "Dad, can you make something for us to play with in the bath? Something that's really cool and really works?"

I rescued an empty cordial bottle from the bin and armed with that, an empty trigger-spray bathroom cleaner bottle, a glue gun and a can of grey undercoat, we started to make our first ever junk model. This sub looks the part and really floats, to get the right effect it's partially filled with stones, sand or gravel from the garden. I dried it out in the oven quickly to sterilise it and stop it going mouldy.

Safety first: When making this kind of toy make sure that containers are thoroughly washed out, no bits can fall off and that there are no sharp corners. Never give a plastic toy you have made to a child under three years of age.

A very easy and quick way to make a great bath toy that really floats

8 years +

40 minutes

Glue gun
Marker
Craft knife
Paint
Plastic cordial bottle
Trigger-spray bottle
  neck

Remove bottle cap and keep, cut off tamper evident ring and discard.

Glue single serving dessert pot to bottle bottom. If the pot has a lip, cut off with a pair of strong kitchen scissors or a craft knife so that pot makes a neat, rounded end to the squash bottle. Make sure that glue goes completely round edge of pot so that the pot is sealed on to the end of the bottle, otherwise water will seep into pot when the submarine is finished and being played with in the bath.

Glue deodorant bottle cap to end of dessert pot to make the submarine prow.

To make coning tower, cut the top part from a kitchen or bathroom pump spray. Use strong kitchen scissors. Mark a straight line on each side and a slightly curved line on the front and back so that the tower will sit nicely on the bottle.

Glue the coning tower to the top of the main hull, making sure that if there are any features in the side of the squash bottle, they are aligned to be horizontal and symmetrical.

Glue a milk poly-bottle cap to the top of the coning tower, so that it is hanging slightly more to the front, to make a deck.

floating submarine

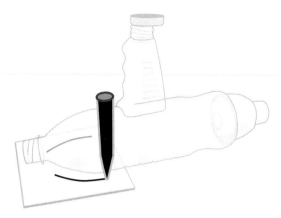

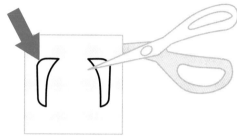

7   To make the tail fins, using any spare flat piece of bottle plastic, trace the profile of the bottle with a marker. To match profile, hold pen vertically and look down from the top. Mark out the shape of the fin and cut out using strong scissors. Cut rounded corners so that fins don't scratch.

8   Using another spare bit of flat plastic bottle side, mark a 70mm diameter circle using a cup or compass, **A**. Draw round the bottle cap, **B**. Draw round the bottle neck, **C**, making sure the circles are concentric.

9   Cut out the disc using strong scissors, although you may need a craft knife to get the inner circle started.

10 Mark eight radial spokes that only go as far as circle **B**.

11 Using strong scissors cut down each spoke and two thirds of the way round each segment on circle **B**. These are the propeller blades, do not cut them off.

12 Twist and bend out each blade in turn, creasing the plastic to make it stay bent.

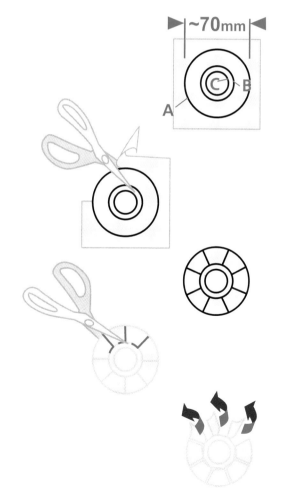

13 In order to float at the correct depth and upright the sub needs ballast. Half fill the submarine with sand or gravel.

15 Glue the tail fins in place, making sure that they are horizontal and level with each other. Glue any other pieces of old plastic or bottle caps to the surface of the submarine hull to add detail as required.

16 Decorate with any suitable waterproof paint. Use spray paint if you have it because it dries quickly and means that you can get on and play with the sub in the bath.

14 Push propeller on to bottle neck and replace cap tightly, but do not glue. Cap can be removed to add or remove ballast at later date. Because propeller is not glued it will be able to rotate.

Why not give the sub a number that is special to you and your children, like your house number or their age, and paint it on the side?

formula one racing car

Do you recognise the cream cleaner bottle? Perhaps it's the special new formula they're using these days, but this container makes a brilliant racing car. The wheels work, the car really rolls, and it also fits a small action figure. We didn't have time to spray our one because the race was about to start, but no doubt you will plan your day better and then you'll have time to adorn it with all manner of sponsors' logos and advertising, just like the real thing.

This Formula One racer cleans up and really rolls

8 years +

1 hour

Glue gun
Marker
Craft knife
Paint
Kitchen cream
  cleaner bottle
1l or 2l milk poly-
  bottle caps
Piece of cardboard
Drinking straws
Tiny piece of packing
  foam sheet
Piece of clear plastic
  bottle
Pen caps or
  chocolate box tray

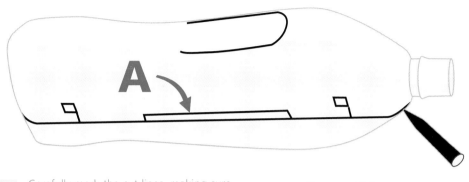

1 Carefully mark the cut lines, making sure that the axle holes are in line so that the axles will be at right angles to the bottle's long axis and will be parallel.

Mark a slot, **A**, as deep as the thick card you are going to use.

4 To make the wheels you will need eight milk poly-bottle caps. Cut square holes or drill only four of the caps in the centre.

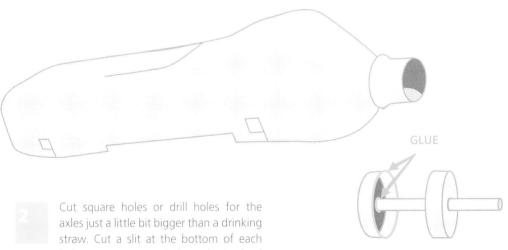

2 Cut square holes or drill holes for the axles just a little bit bigger than a drinking straw. Cut a slit at the bottom of each hole so you can get the axle / wheel assemblies in.

3 Only cut a C shape for the cockpit so you can bend the bottle down to make the seat back.

GLUE

5 Glue a straw on to the underside of the undrilled cap, making sure that it is central and straight.

When the glue has set, pass a drilled cap over the straw and glue round the rim.

formula one racing car

6 Offer the wheel up to the car body and mark the correct length of the straw. Allowing for the other wheel, cut the straw to length and repeat steps 4 and 5 for the other wheel. Repeat for the second axle.

7 Cut a piece of thick card to fit the slot, **A**, and form the floor of the car and the bottom of the side fuel tank bulge.

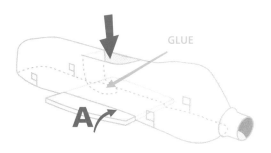

GLUE

A

8 Fold down the cockpit flap and glue to the floor to make seat and seat back.

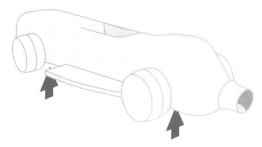

9 Snap fit wheel axle assemblies into place.

10 Cut a piece of thick card to make the front spoiler, upper parts of the fuel tank, side bulges and wing mirrors and glue in to place.

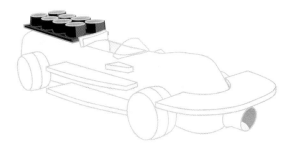

11 Cut a crescent-shaped windshield from a piece of clear soda bottle and glue round cockpit front.

12 To make engine, use a piece of chocolate selection box, or some old pen caps stuck on a piece of card, markered or sprayed black.

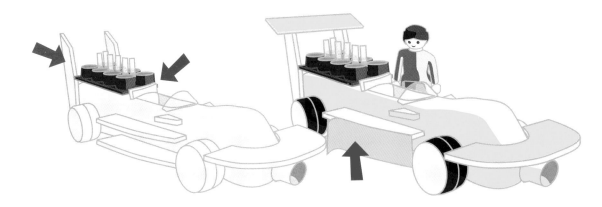

13 For the exhaust pipes, cut six short pieces from some drinking straws and stick in two rows on the top of the engine block.

14 Glue a tiny piece of packing foam to the front of the engine as a head rest.

15 To make the rear spoiler, cut thick cardboard in to two identical short strips and angle tops. Glue to side of body. **NOTE:** You might need a card spacer, depending on the size of the engine part.

16 Cut a rectangle of card to make the rear spoiler and glue on top of the uprights. Glue a strip of paper to the pieces of card on the top and bottom of the fuel tank bulge to complete. Colour the cardboard bits and take the wheels off and spray them black if you want a more authentic look.

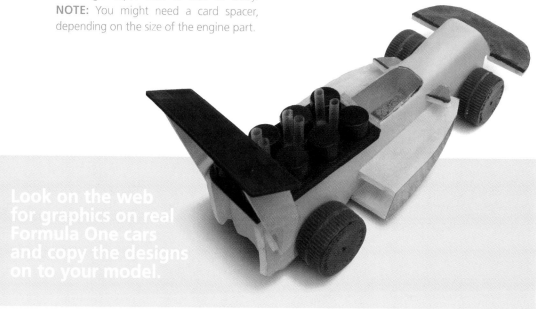

Look on the web for graphics on real Formula One cars and copy the designs on to your model.

helicopter

A nice complicated model for when you have a whole afternoon to occupy. The main rotor turns and the wire coathanger skid-supports flex really nicely when you land it.

You probably won't have exactly the same containers as we did, but making a model from junk is all about discovery, improvisation, problem solving, and working with what is available. With a model like this you most likely find you are doing most of the work, but your kids will love finding suitable things for the next bit you are making, or suggesting solutions when stuff doesn't look right.

Some of the ideas in this project will be helpful whatever type of chopper you make; the way the rotor is put together, how to make a decent-looking tail, how to make the skids – the rest, however, is up to you. The main thing is to start with something nice and chunky for the body and attach the rest on to that.

Make this superb helicopter – it's satisfyingly big and the main rotors turn

14 years +

4 hours

Glue gun
Marker
Craft knife
Paint
Card
Coathanger
Pliers
Assorted bottles and
   tubs

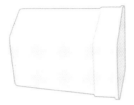

1 Choose a carton or make a box that fits the width of a cream cleaner bottle.

2 Cut a cream cleaner bottle in half and glue gun it into the bottom of the open end of the box.

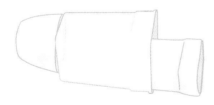

3 Glue a single portion dessert pot on the end of the box.

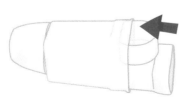

4 Cut the top off a clear salad or dips pot and insert it into gap at top of open end of main carton body, then glue on to cream cleaner bottle.

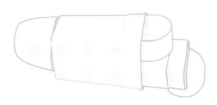

5 Cut a segment out of a washing liquid ball and glue gun to the end of the cream cleaner bottle.

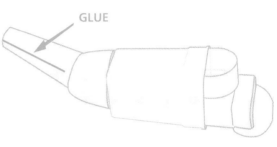

GLUE

6 To make the tail, cut a toilet roll lengthways and roll it down thinner, to make a slight cone. Glue gun it together and then glue on to single portion dessert pot at a slight angle.

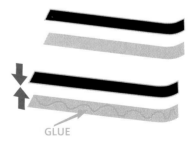

GLUE

7 To make skis use two pieces of cardboard. Bend them up in a curve and glue them together for added strength and so that they stay curved.

helicopter

GLUE

8 Using pliers, bend two pieces of coathanger to form the undercarriage and glue gun them to the skis.

11 To make the main rotor, cut rotor blades from a piece of card, and glue coathanger wire through a bottle top, so that it can rotate. Poke wire through rotor, cover end of wire with a cut down pen cap. Glue coathanger wire strips from top of rotor to pen cap. Glue whole assembly to dessert top.

9 Put more glue-gun glue over the wires and cover the ends with small pieces of slightly curved card to make a really firm fixture.

12 To make the tail rotor assembly, cut rotor from a piece of card, glue it to a 2l milk carton lid and glue the assembled part on to tail. Cut stabilising fin from card and glue at right angles to the tail on the opposite side. Cap the end of the tail with a sliced off washing-up bottle cap.

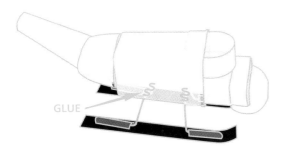

GLUE

10 Glue the main body of the helicopter to the top of the undercarriage, making sure that it is level as the glue sets (glue-gun glue will take up to 60 seconds to set).

13 Glue rotor assembly to top of main body.

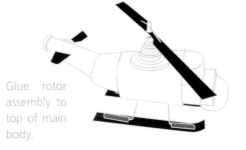

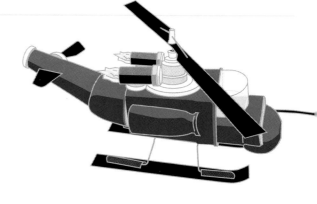

14 To make the engines, slit a toilet roll lengthways then cut in half, roll up tighter and glue with glue gun. Cap one end with a single portion bottle cap, crumple wrapping paper or tin foil and glue in the other end, glue the assembly to a milk carton lid. Make two of these.

16 Cut single dose miniature yoghurt bottle in half lengthways and stick one half on each side of the main body. Glue other pieces of plastic, strips or small bits to various parts of the helicopter to add detail.

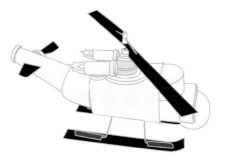

17 Finally, paint your model. If you use spray paint it is a good idea to mask the cockpit windscreen with a bit of masking tape or sticky tape. Once it is painted, decorate further with a black permanent marker.

15 Glue engines to top of main body just behind the rotor assembly. If you have a wider body or longer engines, they can go either side of the rotor assembly.

TIP: paint some of the components before assembling them to get a really good effect.

canoe

It looks the part, fits a small action figure, and I only wish it fitted me! I hear canoes are quite expensive, but this one certainly wasn't.

This is the sort of model that you can make in a few minutes when the kids are bored and want something to do. In essence it is very, very simple, because it is made out of two shower gel bottles glued together, neck to neck. A couple of little bits of detail finish it off, like the splash-guard and the seat, but really this is a 10 to 20 minute project. Next time you buy shower gel, shampoo or conditioner, have a look at all the bottle shapes on offer. All you need for this project is a bottle that stands on its cap, is vaguely symmetrical and has a rounded end. It's not rocket science … it's junk model-making canoe science!

A canoe made from two shower gel bottles, what could be more perfect for the bath?

8 years +

1 hour

Glue gun
Marker
Craft knife
Paint
2 x shower gel
  bottles
Shampoo or
  conditioner bottle
Plastic bottle
Polystyrene fruit tray
Wooden coffee
  stirrers or lolly
  sticks
OPTIONAL:
Short piece of string
  or bootlace

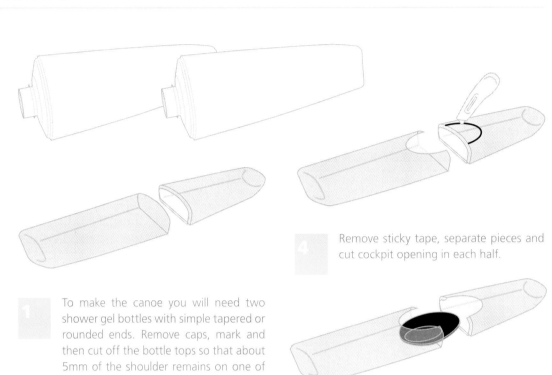

4 Remove sticky tape, separate pieces and cut cockpit opening in each half.

1 To make the canoe you will need two shower gel bottles with simple tapered or rounded ends. Remove caps, mark and then cut off the bottle tops so that about 5mm of the shoulder remains on one of them but not on the other. You will use this to make a strong join when you glue the ends together.

5 Cut the base from an expanded polystyrene fruit tray and glue into one half of the canoe, making sure to leave room at the bottom edge for the other half of the canoe and shoulder to fit in.

2 Without glue, push the ends together and hold in place with sticky tape.

3 To make the splash guard deck top, cut the top shoulder from an oval shampoo or hair conditioner bottle (or similar) that is no wider than the shower gel bottles you are using. Tape in place and using as a guide mark the size of the cockpit opening.

6 Apply glue round the shoulder ridge and push both ends of the canoe together. If you are unsure that you have a watertight join, wait till the glue has set (60 secs) and then apply a bead of glue round the join from the outside.

canoe

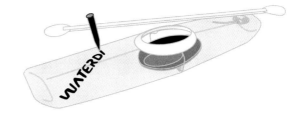

7 Glue the splash deck guard over the cockpit opening to finish off neatly (optional).

8 Make the paddle from coffee stirrers or lolly sticks with a small piece of brightly coloured plastic bottle cut to paddle shape glued at each end.

9 Name, decorate with marker pen and spray if required.

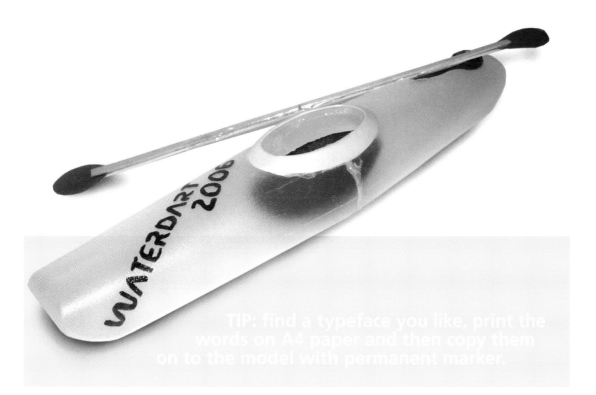

TIP: find a typeface you like, print the words on A4 paper and then copy them on to the model with permanent marker.

steam train

A magnificent wood-burning steam locomotive with real rolling wheels

12 years +

2 hours

Bottle caps
Thick and thin cardboard
Coathanger wire
Glue-gun glue (ideally)
Set of compasses
Single serving drinks bottle
Black and one colour paint (ideally spray paint)

Looking every inch like something that you'd buy from an expensive toy shop, this beautiful train is as satisfying to make as it is fun to play with.

These instructions include templates to trace over for the basic chassis and the cabin as well as measurements for all the important parts. However, given that this model is made from junk, you'll also have to use your inventiveness where your parts aren't exactly the same as mine. That said, don't limit yourself to what junk packaging you have left over in the cupboard. If you want to start this project but you haven't collected up the right bottles and lids, just buy the ones you want next time you go to the supermarket – that way you can get exactly the bottle shape and size you need. The best products for shape are personal care and bath products, shower gels and soap-dispensing bottles.

Be adventurous – have a go at making this wonderful model, perfect for hours of fun and enjoyment.

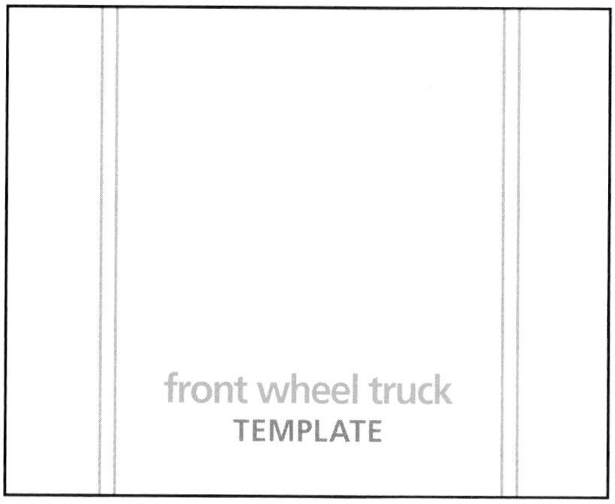

steam train

front wheel truck
TEMPLATE

NOTE: When starting a model the scale is one of the hardest things to judge, especially when you are using junk components. As your parts may differ from the ones used for this model, use these templates, and the dimensions given in the project, as a guide.

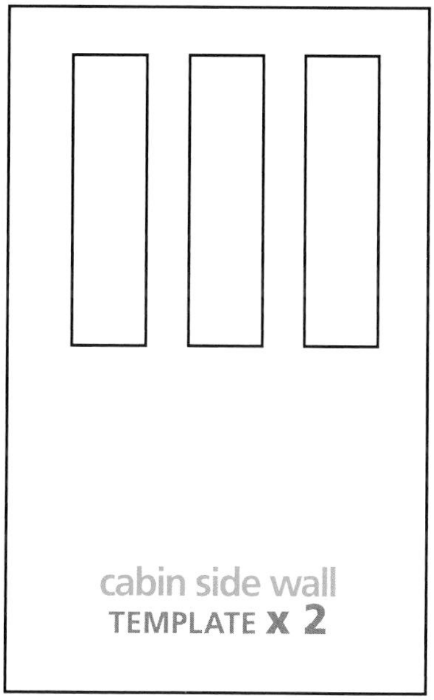

cabin front wall **TEMPLATE**

cabin side wall
TEMPLATE x 2

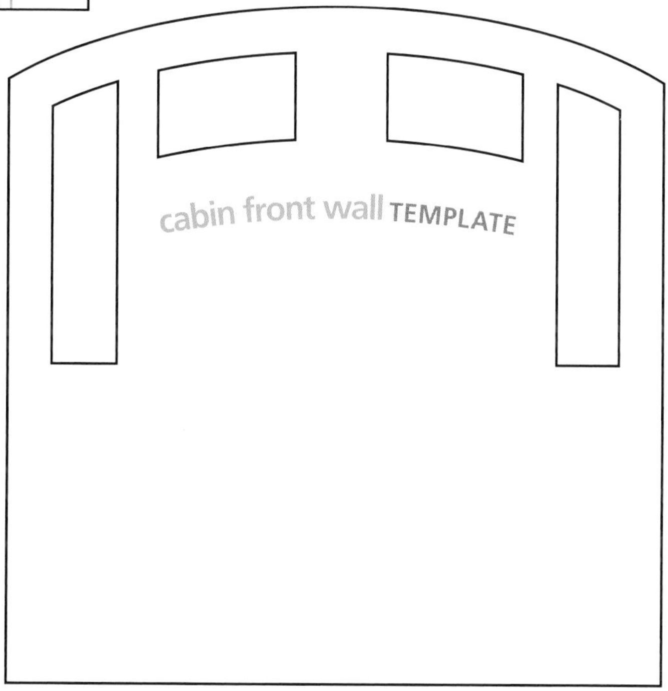

rear wheel truck **TEMPLATE**

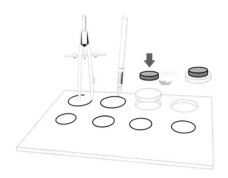

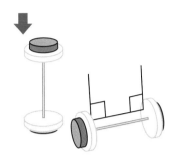

For this project you will need four large wheels and four small ones. For the large wheels use poly-bottle milk lids with diameter 40mm (or similar), and for the small wheels, use fizzy drink bottle lids, diameter 30mm. Draw four circles at 50mm diameter and four at 38mm diameter, on some thick card (foamboard is perfect) cut out and then glue the lids centrally, one to each disc.

If you don't have any bottle caps, you can cut the middle disc of each wheel out of the same cardboard.

Like real train wheels, this is a fixed axle design. Cut four lengths of straight coat hanger wire about 85mm long. To make each wheel pair, push one end of a wire length through the cardboard side of the wheel. Remove it and then put the nozzle of the glue gun up to the hole and squeeze in a little bit of glue-gun glue. Push the wire axle in fully.

Do the same at the other end of the wire so that you have two wheels glued securely on the axle. Make sure that the wheels are at right angles to each other. Repeat for the other big and small wheels until you have four sets of wheels and axles.

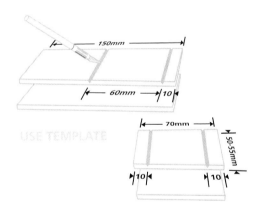

To make the wheel trucks, cut two sets of two rectangular pieces of thick cardboard. The width of the cardboard should just fit between the wheels so that they don't rub. The width will depend on the size of lid you used for the wheels and the thickness of your cardboard. In one small bit and one large bit make two crosswise channels (spaced apart as shown). Either cut a V-shaped groove or crush the cardboard in with the back of a dinner knife. Do no cut all the way through. Only make grooves in one set of the rectangles.

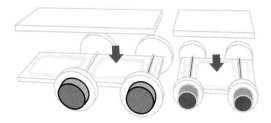 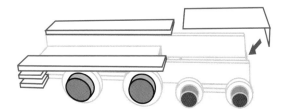

5 Carefully glue round the parts with the grooves in, making sure not to get the glue in the grooves, and then rest the wheel assemblies in the grooves and stick the matching bits of card over the top. This will trap the wheel assemblies but still allow them to rotate freely.

7 Now you have the basic running gear assembly you can start to build up the locomotive parts. Cut two long thin rectangles of thick card that extend to just cover the big wheels and glue them on to the top of the chassis. Cut four small rectangles of thick card and glue them behind the big wheels (these will be the driver's steps). Use two on each side. Finally cut a piece of thin card only as wide as the chassis and use it to box in the part over the small wheels.

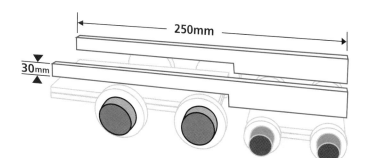

6 Join the two wheel trucks with thick cardboard, shaped as shown. Cut two rectangles of thick cardboard about 250mm long and about 60mm wide. Rest the wheels on a level surface and cut a step in the card so that you can glue it to both sets of wheels. Make sure that when the cardboard is glued to the base it stands higher than the big wheels. To do this, the width of the cardboard at the big wheel end should not be less than 30mm, although its actual size depends on the size of wheels that you have chosen.

8 Spray the whole assembly black. Don't spray too thickly all at once, or you will gum up the wheels. Three or four light coats of spray from all angles should be enough, making sure that the wheels still turn after each coat.

▶

Use a large, straight sided personal care or soap pump dispenser bottle for the boiler. If you don't have the right one at home, buy a cheap one and decant the contents into another bottle. Mark round the bottle so that your cut will be at right angles to the axis of the bottle and neatly cut with strong scissors.

11 Rest the boiler on to the wheel chassis and position the funnel in the best place and carefully mark round it on the boiler.

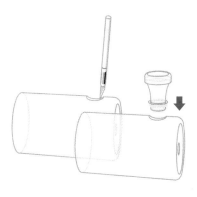

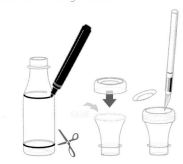

10 To make the funnel, mark then cut the top and base off a single serving drink bottle. At the top, cut slightly past the shoulder so that the top fits snugly in the base part. Turn over, apply glue to the cut rim of the top and glue inside the base. When set carefully cut a circular hole from the base part to make the funnel opening. **Take care**, the base of a bottle is the toughest part of the plastic, and it is easy to slip and cut yourself if you are pressing hard.

12 Carefully cut out the hole for the funnel base. Check that the funnel fits and adjust the hole as necessary. You'll see that the top of the bottle that you used for the funnel has a flange round it, this will form a nice finish when the funnel is inserted. Apply glue to the funnel and push into the hole in the top of the boiler.

13 Glue a smaller rounded bottle cap in place behind the funnel and then paint the boiler and funnel. Spray is best, and if you used clear bottles, spray inside for a lovely glossy finish.

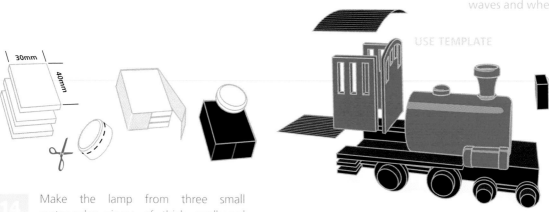

USE TEMPLATE

14 Make the lamp from three small rectangular pieces of thick cardboard glued together. For a neat finish, cover the edges with thin card or paper and paint or spray the finished block black. To make the light, cut a thin slice off the top of a white or clear single serving drinks bottle and glue to the block.

16 Glue the boiler and drive pistons in place, so that the pistons are level with the front of the boiler and rest up against the front of the walk-boards. Glue the lamp in place. Cut the cabin out of thick card using the templates as a guide. For a neat finish, paint the cabin before you glue it to the locomotive assembly.

Use a piece of thin card for the curved roof, cut out so that it overhangs by a small amount at the front and sides and as far as the back of the locomotive at the back. Lastly, use thin cardboard to make the cabin floor to fit inside the cabin, paint and glue in place.

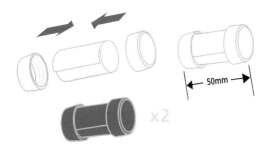

15 Make two drive pistons, one for each side, using a rolled up piece of thin card or plastic glued at each end into a single serving drinks bottle cap. Paint or spray the same colour as the boiler.

17 Add detail and decorate as much as you want. Stick black straws to the sides of the boiler as guide rails, and at the join between the boiler and chassis to hide any glue blobs. Stick thin pieces of card to the cabin side as trim and anything else you can think of.

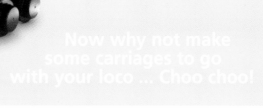

Now why not make some carriages to go with your loco ... Choo choo!

Accurately measure time using sand and two drinks bottles

Nowadays, hourglasses are used almost entirely for decorative purposes because much more accurate ways of measuring time have been invented. Nevertheless, this great little experiment results in a durable and dynamic model that is as fascinating to watch as it is fun to build and talk about.

12 years +

2 hours

Single serving drink bottles
Small piece of plastic
Fine sand
Sandpaper

People have been using the flow of sand to measure the passing hours of the day since the time of the Egyptians. From about the 15th century onwards, sand-filled hourglasses were being used by just about anybody who could afford one.

During Magellan's pioneering voyage to circumnavigate the world, each ship kept as many as 18 hourglasses, and it was the job of a ship's page to turn the hourglasses to provide times for the ship's log. In this project, you'll see how easy it is to make a sand timer that can be used to accurately measure the time needed to boil an egg. Use soft, fine, dry sand, calibrate your timer carefully and it will accurately measure the three minutes it takes to cook a perfect soft-boiled egg.

Building an egg timer combines proper science with all the fun of a making project your kid can have an active role in. On p121 you'll find an experimental discussion outline with a few key interesting facts designed to help boost your children's interest and explain simply what's going on in the experiment.

Drill a small hole (about 1mm to 2mm in diameter, depending on the grade of sand you're using) in the centre of the bottle cap. Use a cordless drill and hold the cap carefully, preferably in a small vice.

Draw round the shoulder of one of the bottles with a marker on to a piece of thin packaging plastic cut from a detergent bottle or something similar.

To calibrate your timer, fill the bottle with sand and screw on the cap with the hole in it and time how long it takes for all the sand to drain out. Add more sand to make it last longer or drill a bigger hole to make it go quicker, until it takes three minutes to drain out.

Holding the plastic sheet carefully, drill a hole in the centre of the drawn circle using the same diameter drill bit as the one you calibrated with in step 2. (Make sure to drill into a piece of scrap wood and not your tabletop). Cut out the circle of plastic and sandpaper both sides.

Put the sand to one side and saw off the threaded part of the bottle just above the shoulder ring. You will need to do this for both bottles. Make sure that the shoulder ring is flat and level. Sandpaper the surface lightly to smooth it off and give a key for the glue.

Fill one of the bottles with the exact amount of sand from your calibration in step 2.

Using quick setting epoxy glue or glue-gun glue round the top of the shoulder of one bottle.

Carefully stick the circle of plastic on to the shoulder making sure that no glue goes inside the bottle or the hole.

9 When the first layer of glue is set, repeat and stick the other bottle upside down, on to the first bottle. Be very careful to make sure that the bottle joins are sealed, but the glue does not flow into the hole.

When was the first recorded use of a sand timer?

The earliest pictures showing the use of the hourglass seems to be in the AD 1338 fresco *Allegory of Good Government* by Ambrogio Lorenzetti.

What is the largest sand timer in the world?

Since 2008, the largest sand timer in the world has been in Red Square in Moscow. It stands nearly 12 metres in height, weighs 40 tonnes and can run for over a year on one turn!

Are sand timers still used in public?

Apart from loads of people using them for fun to time egg-boiling and as simple timers in board games, both houses of the Australian Parliament still use three hourglasses to time certain procedures, such as divisions (the time taken to take a vote on a question).

What is an hourglass figure?

The shape of the hourglass with its bulge at top and bottom and a narrow part in the middle gave its name to the look of the painful corset worn by women to give them a silhouette resembling the hourglass shape: wide bottom, narrow waist and wide top.

Reliable routines

When parents split up, their children's routines are often the first casualty. New routines need to be set up quickly, and here are ten top ideas on how to go about it.

As we get older, we are told that routine is something to avoid, a numbing thing that saps our creativity, stifles our energy and will dull our lustre if we let it. But like it or not, routine is something that we all need a bit of. It is the framework that provides us the security to step out and be creative when we want to. For kids life without routine is very frightening and confusing. When parents split up their children's routines are the first casualty. New routines need to be set up quickly. They act as a cushion for the emotional turmoil that surrounds a family breakdown and provide a set of reliable reference points for everyone involved.

For dads who suddenly find themselves seeing less of their children than they would like, setting up some structure can make life a lot more bearable. Dads are good at starting these routines, the best of which grow into family traditions or etch themselves into our memories as happy times we spent together.

Here are some routines that will hopefully inspire you and give you ideas about things to do with your children to show them that whatever happens they can always rely on you.

1 Phone your children at the same time every day or each week

Where possible arrange with your ex-partner that you will ring the children at the same time each day. If the children are young, stick religiously to the routine. If ringing each day is not possible, then fix the best day or days each week and always call at the agreed time. Wherever you are, make time to do it so your children can rely on you ringing. Sometimes they won't say much more than goodnight, other times they will chat away about all the things that they have done that day.

2 When you pick your children up, use the same distinctive knock or doorbell ring

Be nice and happy when you pick up your children, whatever is said to you or has been said between you and your ex-partner beforehand. You want to make sure that your children don't get to associate your knock at the door or ring on the doorbell with unhappy times. A special ring or knock to signal your arrival will establish a picking-up routine that your children will start to look forward to.

3 Go to the bakery on your way back from picking your kids up and buy a bun each

The smell of fresh bread is lovely and everything feels better when you have some food inside you. If you don't live near a bakery, buy hot cross buns beforehand and then toast them the minute you get in.

4 Have and play a favourite tape, CD, or iPod playlist in the car

Choose tracks with your children or let them pick favourite ones that you can all sing along together to. Make sure that they are upbeat songs.

5 Always make the same favourite meal on the same day of the week

Make sure it is a healthy and tasty meal that your children like and then you know that they will look forward to it.

6 Set aside a time to do homework each week

At first this might seem like a chore, but get it right and you'll find yourself spending some real quality time with your children as you sit with them and help them through their homework. Not only do you get to see what they are doing at school, but later you know that when they are at school, they will be reminded of the bond between you when they hand in their homework.

7 Set aside one night every month as a home film night

Rent out that old favourite or the latest release, get a bar of chocolate or some popcorn and make a fun routine out of it.

8 Read to your children at bedtime

Cosy in their beds, warm, happy, relaxed and listening to their dad read them a story, what kid could ask for more? What a lovely routine to look forward to. Get

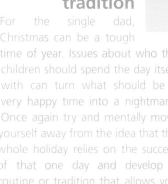

into a good book and you'll be looking forward to the next chapter as much as they are.

9 Set up a birthday routine

Routines don't have to be just about what you do each week, yearly routines are just as important. Children whose parents have separated can't spend every birthday day with their mum AND dad. Learn how to be relaxed about this, and don't put too much emphasis on The Day. If you can arrange it, alternate the years, if not, don't make it a battlefield. Set up a nice birthday routine, a restaurant meal, or a special celebratory trip out. Make it a thing you can do each year, and stick to it. Next year will come around soon enough, and before you know it you will have a wonderful birthday tradition to look forward to.

10 Set up a Christmas time tradition

For the single dad, Christmas can be a tough time of year. Issues about who the children should spend the day itself with can turn what should be a very happy time into a nightmare. Once again try and mentally move yourself away from the idea that the whole holiday relies on the success of that one day and develop a routine or tradition that allows you to spread the happiness of the season across other days too. Make Christmas stockings with your children with their initial on, and take your time over them so that they can keep them and bring them out again next year.

steam train PAGE 112

I cannot think of any need in childhood as strong as the need for a father's protection.

DR SIGMUND FREUD
Father of psychology

Children don't need much to fire up their imaginations, and are desperate to participate in the fictional universes of their favourite game and story characters. These Great Adventures projects play to this need by adding imaginary backstories to each plan, turning the projects into voyages of discovery and providing a starting point for the richest possible interaction with each craft activity.

dragonhide valuables pouch PAGE 129

feather quills PAGE 146

GROWING A CRYSTAL

being there
HELP YOUR KIDS BE CREATIVE – PART ONE

dragon hunter's goggles PAGE 153

dragon-egg pendant

Hide your dragon's eggs from prying eyes

8 years +

45 minutes
(incl. glue drying)

Dowelling
Hacksaw
Paint (that dries
waterproof)
Small metal
screw eye
Sandpaper
Glue-gun glue

Each morning after breakfast, I set aside two hours to attend to my post bag. I call it 'my armchair adventuring', because never a day goes by when I am not somehow transported to a distant realm by the opening of an envelope. On one such occasion I received a letter from an experienced explorer called Melros. The letter contained four miniature dragon's eggs which, although harmless-looking enough, had caused her considerable problems. Melros had disguised them as pendants, but when that failed to stop the unwanted interest, she sent them to me for safe keeping.

An hour or two in the library revealed that these were extremely rare and fine examples of petrified Wisp Dragon eggs. As I know how interested you are in such diversions, I hereby provide you the instructions needed to make replicas, so that you can own one or two of these exquisite pieces for yourself. They make charming pendants and will never fail to elicit a comment or two from admirers each time they are worn.

dragon-egg pendant

1 Use 10 to 12mm dowel and mark about 25mm lengths for each mini dragon's egg you want to make.

4 Screw a small metal eye into the centre of one end. It might help to make a small hole to start with, using a nail.

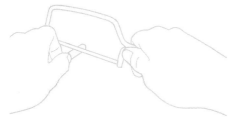

2 Use a hacksaw to saw the dowel to length (hold the longer end). This is good sawing practice for kids as it is easy and safe to use a hacksaw.

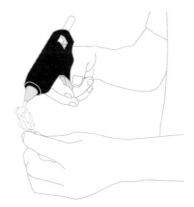

3 Sandpaper the corners off to make the ends rounded like an egg.

5 Holding the metal eye apply a thin trickle of glue-gun glue in an organic pattern, over the surface of the egg.

6 Put sticky tape either side of the metal eye as a mask and a handle and paint the egg in your chosen colour with waterproof paint.

▶

7 To distress, paint on a layer of darker acrylic thinned with water.

9 When dry, carefully paint silver or gold paint on the glue gun lines.

10 Thread on to a necklace chain, gold thread or yarn to make an attractive necklace.

8 Before the paint dries wipe off with a cloth, leaving some paint in the cracks.

Wear your pendant out and you are guaranteed admiring glances – but be careful of those Wisp Dragons, they want their eggs back!

dragonhide valuables pouch

Dragonhide is a remarkable material, its surface hardness is comparable to that of quartz, and in the past it was rendered workable only with specialist tools tipped with topaz, corundum or diamond. In the late 19th century, centres capable of tanning dragonhide existed in a few countries, but if one desired the most superb workmanship, material of the highest quality, and security of supply, then only the tanneries in Mongolia's capital, the City of Felt, would suffice.

Apparently, dragonhide is still widely available and these days equipment exists that permits you to make accessories like this exquisite pouch. I have had Collinworth draw up some simple instructions, which I'm certain you will be able to follow, should the mood take you.

Once the top of this valuables pouch is pulled shut, only the nimblest fingers will be able to loosen the cord, thus it will keep all manner of treasure safe from theft and misadventure.

A magnificent dragonhide accessory that will keep all your valuables safe

10 years +

15 minutes

Scissors
Glue gun
Soft fabric
String or cord

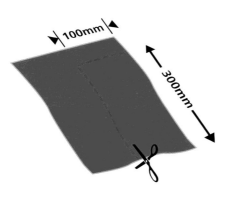

1 Cut out a rectangle of velour, felt or velvet fabric about 300mm by 100mm.

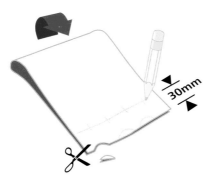

2 Fold the fabric over face-side in and cut about four small scallops out of the cut edge. Mark a line across the fabric to get the hole positions neatly aligned.

3 Fold the fabric over at the marked line and cut out four small holes by cutting semi-circles across the fold. Repeat at the other end.

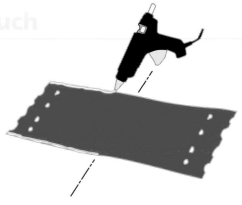

4 Place face up and put a thin stripe of glue-gun glue as close to the edge as you can, halfway down both sides (as shown).

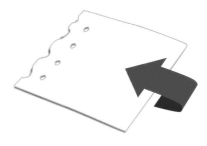

5 Fold the fabric over making certain to keep it square, and flatten out. Wait for two minutes until the glue has cooled and set.

6 Turn the bag right-side out and then carefully dribble glue-gun glue stripes diagonally across the fabric surface. Crisscross them to give a diamond pattern. Do both sides the same.

dragonhide valuables pouch

7 When the glue has set either paint gold on to the glue strips or use antique finger polish to highlight the glue stripes. You can use silver, any metallic paint or even black if you don't have gold.

9 Using another piece of the same cord, thread through in the same fashion but starting from the other side.

Now when you pull the two knotted ends apart, the bag should close tightly.

If it doesn't stay closed, you may have to thread the cords back on themselves one more time.

8 Thread cord or elastic braid through the holes, in for the first hole and then out and in till you have gone all round the neck of the bag. Tie off the cord in a simple knot.

The perfect carry-case for your valuables, or even your spectacles

wizard's wand

Cast a craft spell as you make this wonderful wand

12 years +

60 minutes
(incl. glue drying)

A4 paper sheet
Double-sided tape
Glue gun
PVA

Of all the magical instruments, none is considered as important, or as useful to the budding witch or wizard, as the wand. The more conservative members of the magical community would have us believe that only those most skilled in the craft of wandmaking can fashion a wand. But having seen a wandsman at work, I have concluded that anyone should easily be able to make a beautiful wand, capable of the most powerful magic.

Another myth I would like to dispel without further ado, is the outdated idea that each wizard or witch may only possess one wand. Some of the world's finest sorcerers, a few of whom I have known personally, have any number of wands, each one capable of a particular form of magic. I knew one eminent spellbinder whose prized wand collection numbered three hundred and sixty six, one for each day of the year including a priceless golden *toverstokje* only to be used on that most magical of days, February 29th.

wizard's wand

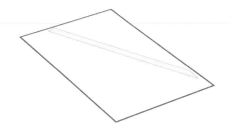

1 Stick a strip of double-sided tape diagonally across a sheet of A4 paper.

5 Trim to give straight ends.

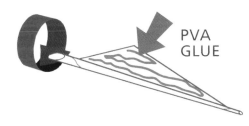

2 Roll the paper up very tightly diagonally allowing one end to be slightly less tight than the other to give a thin tapered roll.

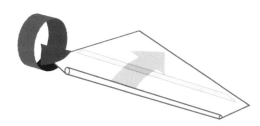

PVA GLUE

3 When you roll over the double-sided tape stop and put a little PVA on the remaining paper.

6 Fill each end with glue-gun glue (one end at a time). Pack the big end with tissue paper if you want to use less glue. The big end may take a couple of goes to plug it completely.

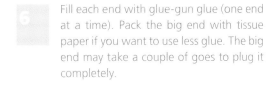

4 Roll tightly and leave to dry for 30 minutes.

7 Turn the wand while applying a glue gun bead to make a nice pattern. Keep turning while it sets (about a minute).

▶

8 Spray the wand with an undercoat or paint with house emulsion to seal.

11 As you are painting wipe off the paint with a damp kitchen wipe to leave dark paint in the cracks and corners.

9 Paint wand with base colour of choice, using acrylic paint that dries permanent. The painting doesn't have to be that even.

12 Rub some gold paint, burnishing paste or gold gel marker on to the raised beads to highlight them.

10 When base coat is dry start painting with thinned wash of black acrylic paint making sure to get it into all the corners.

Use bits of wood or bark to trim your wand, and string or even cooked spaghetti instead of glue for the patterning.

wand box

A wand-box maker's craft is an exacting one. In order for it to perform its duties, the wand box must be made to precise dimensions, and none but the best boxes are capable of containing a wand's magic in its most potent state.

The wand box is typically made from enchanted cardboard of between 2mm and 5mm in thickness. Tradition requires that the box is covered with a thin, but good quality paper (or, for expensive wands, silk fabric), and that the base and lid of the wand box be covered in contrasting colours. In the example shown here, the established wandmakers have used their preferred combination of silver and black, but you may use your taste and judgment to choose any suitable colours. Specialty papers exist for covering board, but any thin paper or gift wrap will do. You can even add a label to finish off your wand box in the most professional way.

Learn the skills of a master wand-box maker to protect and display your wand in style

10 years +

60 minutes

Glue gun
Coloured paper
Thick card
Double-sided tape
Craft knife

download available

wand box

BOX DIMENSIONS FORMULA

base	lid
Width = 70mm	Width = 70mm + (2 x CT)
Depth = 30mm	Depth = 30mm + (1 x CT)
Length = WL + 30mm	Length = WL + 30mm + (2 x CT)

WL = Wand Length   CT = Card Thickness

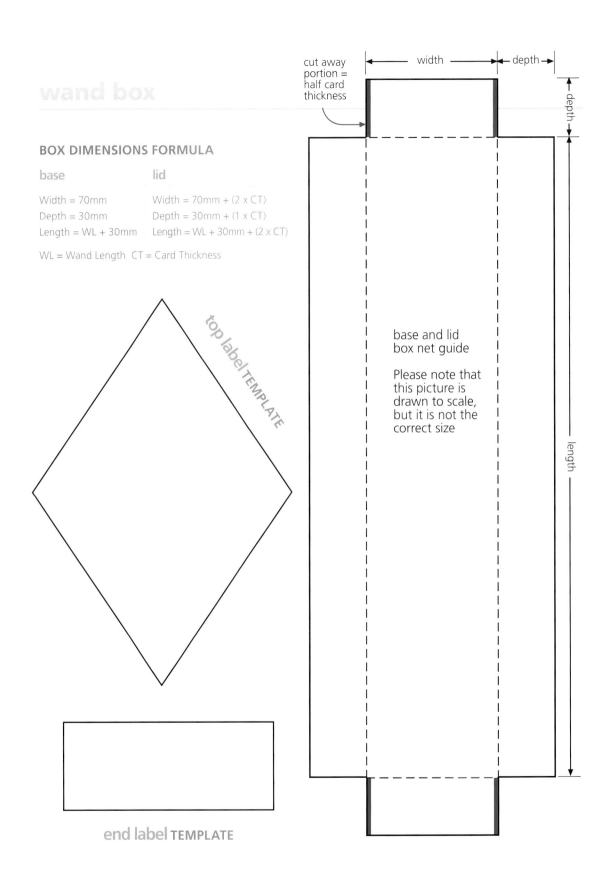

cut away portion = half card thickness

width

depth

depth

top label TEMPLATE

base and lid box net guide

Please note that this picture is drawn to scale, but it is not the correct size

length

end label TEMPLATE

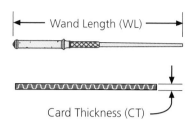

Wand Length (WL)

Card Thickness (CT)

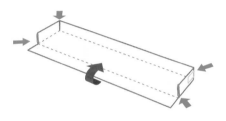

1 Measure your wand length in millimetres and measure your card thickness in millimetres. Using the formula on the template sheet work out the dimensions for the box base and lid.

4 Using a sharp craft knife, carefully cut out the base box net. Crease the cardboard deeply. If it is thick corrugated board you might have to make a V-shaped crease with the handle end of a teaspoon.

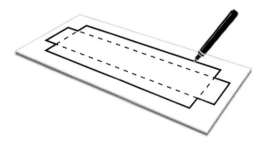

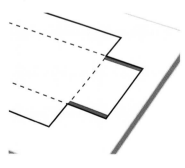

2 The box base and lid both start out as a cross shape made from five long rectangles. The centre rectangle is the shape that will need to be creased.

5 Put glue down each corner and fold up the sides. You can secure the box with clear sticky tape.

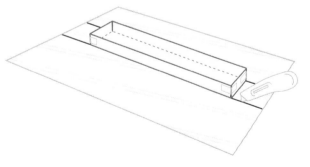

3 To make sure that the box folds up squarely you will also need to remove a small bit on the side of each end tab. Remove a strip, half a card thickness wide on each side.

6 Coat your cover paper in double-sided tape, or spray glue (you can use white glue, but you will have to proceed one face at a time). Glue the box to the middle of the paper and cut four slits from the corners as shown.

▶

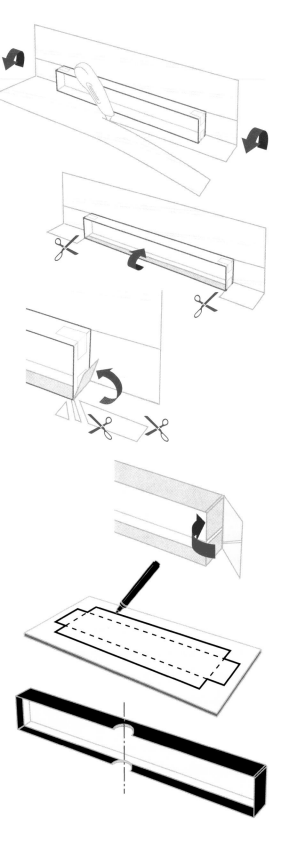

7 Roll the box over and glue the side on, then trim off the paper so that there is enough to fold over the box edge and about 10mm to 15mm down the inside of the box.

8 Cut a slit at the corners as shown and then neatly wrap the paper over the edge and down inside the box.

9 Depending on the thickness of your cardboard you might have to cut some little strips at the sides as shown. Cut these and tuck over and then fold round the remaining piece to partially cover the end of the box. Repeat for the other long side.

10 To finish the end nicely fold the remaining piece over the end and down inside.

11 Using the formula from the template sheet calculate the dimensions of the lid then mark out and repeat the instructions 3–10. Cover the top in a colour that contrasts with the base.

12 When the top is covered use a sharp craft knife to cut two semicircular cutouts in the box lid side halfway along it.

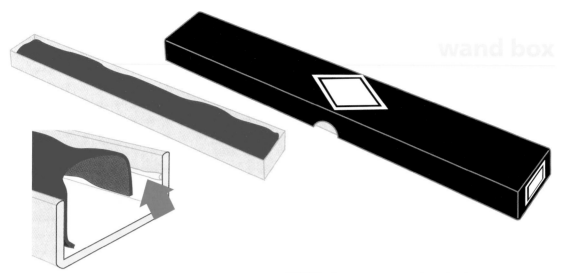

wand box

13 Line the box with smart fabric. You can use felt or velvet if you have some. Cut the fabric so that it is about twice as wide and a little bit longer than the box base. Use fabric glue or glue-gun glue and working a bit at a time, run a bead of glue down the inside of the box side and glue the outside of the fabric to it. Work on one side first and then when the glue is dry do the same for the other side so that when you are finished the glued part can't be seen. Just tuck the ends round and secure with a little blob of glue.

14 Trace over or download our special templates from the website and cut out the main label and two end labels. Glue them in position as shown. Fill in the blank labels with your name or the type of wand and its core. Write neatly, you are now a master wand-box builder!

A wand box specification form and labels make the perfect finishing touches. Go to our website to print them out.

secret box book

This box looks just like a beautiful antique book, and is perfect for hiding away your secrets

11 years +

2 hours

Craft knife
Glue-gun glue
White glue
Paint (brown, black and gold)
Embossed wallpaper
Gold and red paper

download available

Once upon a time, not so long ago, the trade in dragons' eggs and other fire-belly related materials was banned. New laws threatened harsh punishments for anyone found in possession of prohibited contraband, but they had little effect. As is often the case, the legislation didn't really stop the sale and transport of the goods, it just pushed it underground. Collectors unwilling to give up their prized dragonolia devised ever cleverer ways of hiding their collections. One of the most favoured hiding places was the hollowed book. Tucked away in a large library, secret box books (as they became known) provided an excellent and readily accessible hiding place for smallish items of high value. I have had Collinworth draw up some plans so that you can make your very own secret box book. The plans are for one of the larger books that I believe will hold objects as broad and as tall as a sheet of office printer paper. Authentic labels, available on our website will complete the box beautifully.

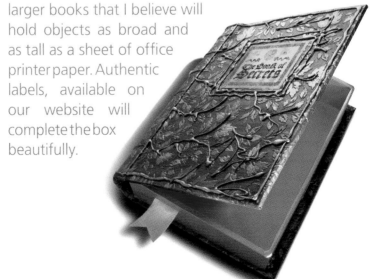

secret box book

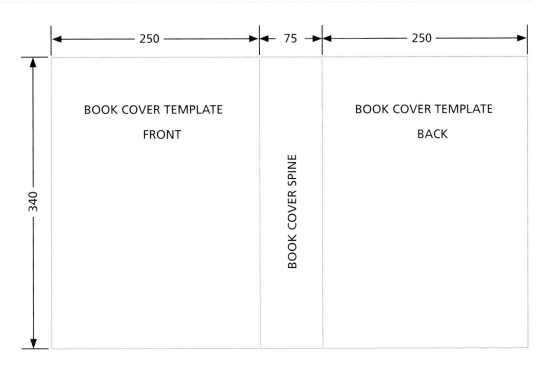

| 250 | 75 | 250 |

BOOK COVER TEMPLATE

FRONT

BOOK COVER SPINE

BOOK COVER TEMPLATE

BACK

340

MARK OUT THESE SHAPES ON SOME THICK (5mm) CORRUGATED CARDBOARD. IF YOUR CARD IS NOT

BIG ENOUGH TO MAKE THE WHOLE BOOK COVER AND SPINE IN ONE PIECE, THEN MAKE IT FROM THREE

SECTIONS AND JOIN THEM TOGETHER WITH A STRIP OF FABRIC GLUED EITHER SIDE OF THE CARD USING WHITE GLUE

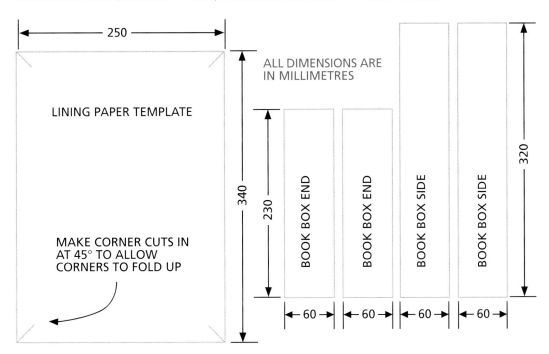

250

LINING PAPER TEMPLATE

MAKE CORNER CUTS IN AT 45° TO ALLOW CORNERS TO FOLD UP

340

ALL DIMENSIONS ARE IN MILLIMETRES

230

BOOK BOX END

BOOK BOX END

BOOK BOX SIDE

BOOK BOX SIDE

320

| 60 | 60 | 60 | 60 |

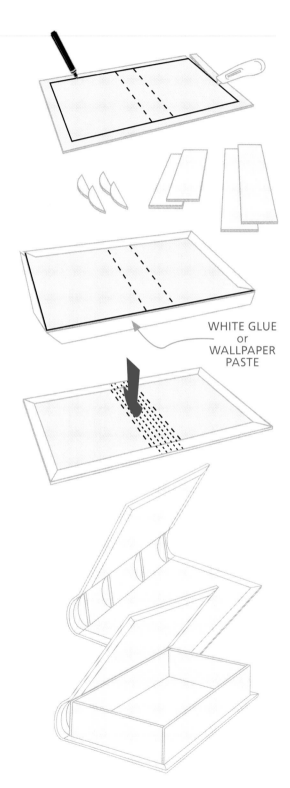

1. Mark out and cut out the book cover using the measurements supplied on the template sheet.

2. Cut out the four crescent shapes using the templates on the label sheet on p144.

3. Wrap the cover in a piece of embossed wallpaper. Wallpaper shops and DIY shops will always give you a small off-cut, so it will be easy to get some. Choose an organic looking pattern; I chose leaves for mine.

WHITE GLUE
or
WALLPAPER
PASTE

4. Crease or score the inside of the spine in straight lines between the spine marks that you made earlier, this will help the spine bend nicely round the crescent shapes.

5. Glue the spine round the little crescent shapes so that they are evenly spaced along the length of the spine. Make sure the two end pieces are inset from the edge of the cover so that you won't be able to see them when the book is finished.

6. Construct the box from the box sides and ends. Glue-gun glue the first side to the base and the flat fronts of the spine crescents and then glue the other three sides on so that they are square and glued to each other and the back cover of the book.

secret box book

7   Use a pencil to mark out a rectangle on the front cover. This should be comfortably bigger than the label template.

8   Using the glue gun to create more pronounced relief, draw over the marked out rectangle and any other features on the embossed wallpaper, like stems or flowers etc.

9   Paint the cover dark brown using water-based emulsion house decorating paint or using spray paint. The paint you use must dry waterproof, otherwise it will wash off in the next step.

10   When the brown paint is dry, mix up some black acrylic paint with a little bit of water and brush on and wipe off. As the black paint stays in all the creases of the pattern, it will make the cover look old. Apply and wipe off until you get the effect you want.

11   When the black paint is dry, use gold, bronze or silver paint or better still, rubbing paste, to rub over and highlight the glue gun strips and the most prominent parts of the embossed wallpaper pattern. Trace over the label template and design your book title, then glue it inside the rectangle.

12   Neatly cover the box / pages edge with gold paper, sticking it on with white glue or better still, double-sided sticky tape. Cover the card so that the top edge is covered and the covering goes a little way down the inside of the box.

▶

secret box book

book label TEMPLATE

crescent spine formers TEMPLATE x 4

60mm

box edge HEIGHT

This is the height of the box sides and the maximum
length of the crescent shapes.

13 Line the inside front cover with a contrasting shade of paper and then line the inside of the box. First line the bottom of the box. Cut out a piece of lining paper with mitre cuts in the corners. Push the paper right down in to the corners.

14 Cut a strip of lining paper slightly smaller than the height of the box sides and line the box sides so that the bottom edge of lining paper and the side edges of gold paper are covered neatly.

15 Make a slit in the box side and push the end of a ribbon through with a blunt dinner knife, fold end over and glue on the inside of the box. Do the same at the top of the box. At the top tuck over and glue down inside the spine for the bottom cut a V-shape out and seal with a dab of white glue to stop it fraying.

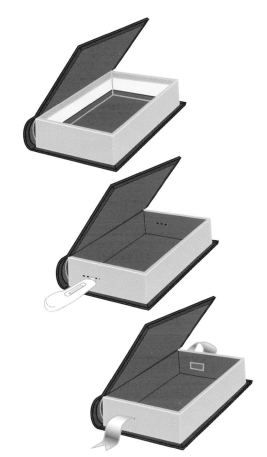

What will you hide inside?

feather quills

Easy to make, these real feather quills are both functional and highly magical

10 years +

1 hour

Ink jet printer
Thick printer paper
Colouring pencils or
felt-tip pens

download available

Henry stared vacantly out of the window, the nib of his quill poised an inch or so above the journal into which he had been busily scratching his version of the day's events. The feather ruffled slightly in the gentle breeze blowing through the open French doors.

"Imagine," he said, cocking his head to one side and tapping the nib on the page so that it made an ink blot, "if one could invent a quill that had everlasting ink."

Henry, my ten-year-old nephew, was staying at the mansion over the summer holidays and I had quickly come to realise that he was given to saying the strangest things. I never forgot that chance comment and decades later, as soon as the first ballpoint pens were available, I put together this little project, which neatly marries the elegance of a feather quill with the practicality and writing convenience of a ballpoint pen. I sincerely hope you enjoy it.

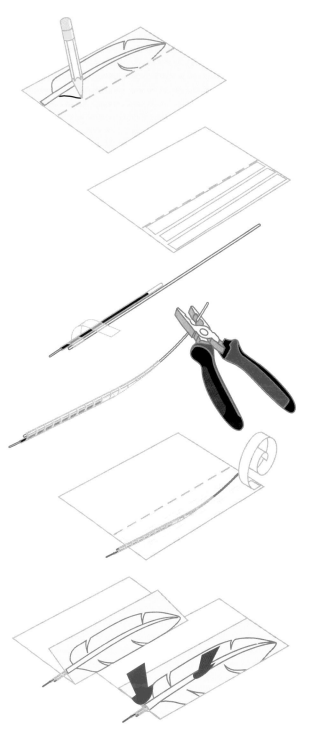

1 Draw a line lengthways down a piece of A4 sized paper about one third of the way across the page. You can use plain paper or brightly coloured gift wrapping paper. Copy or trace the outline of the feather that you want to make from the patterns supplied, or make up your own feather shape.

2 Turn the paper over and put double-sided sticky tape all over the part of the sheet where you drew the feather.

3 Take the thin cartridge out of a cheap click button ballpoint pen (the writing tip must be one of the thinnest ones) and tape it to a straight piece of coathanger wire.

4 Bend the coathanger to match the gentle curve of the stem (or rachis, to give it its proper name). Lay it on the drawing you made and cut it to length with a pair of pliers.

5 Peel off the double-sided tape and position the pen-wire part over the stem. Note: It is much easier to see through the paper if you hold it up against a window or another light source.

6 Fold the feather over along one of its edges and then carefully press the paper down round the pen-wire part to make the stem budge out down the middle, so it looks just like a real feather.

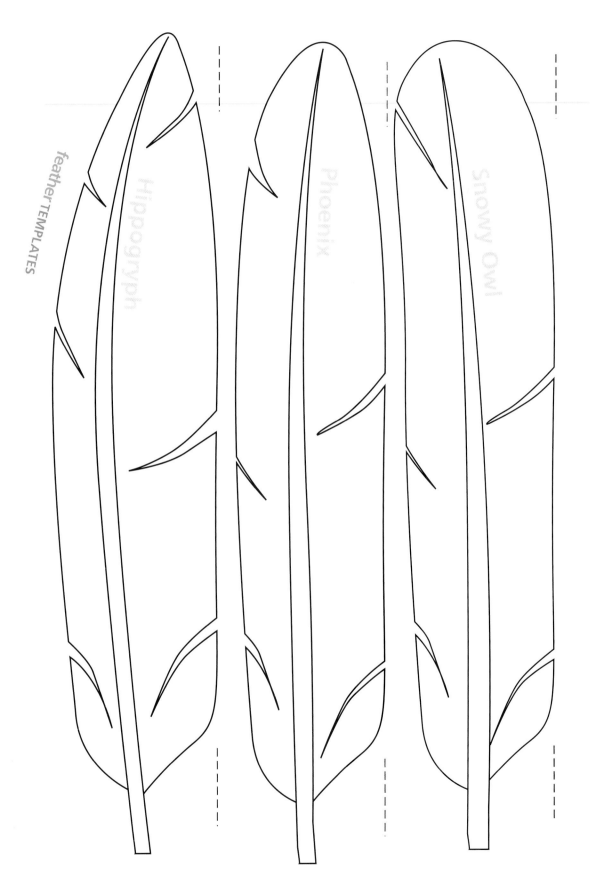

feather TEMPLATES

Hipogryph

Phoenix

Snowy Owl

feather quills

7 Paint or spray the feather on both sides. Use bright colours. Look in a picture book or search on the web to give you some ideas of the sort of beautiful markings bird feathers have. You can paint over your line, but make sure that you can still see it, so that you have something to guide you when you come to cut it out.

8 Carefully cut round the feather outline.

9 Wrap some clear tape round the bottom of the feather stem and round the pen end to secure the pen in place and give you something to grip when you write with it.

Phoenix, Snowy Owl and Hippogryph coloured quill designs are available to print from our website.

magical ink pot

What more useful partner to the quill could there be than a magical ink pot?

12 years +

20 minutes

A4 paper sheet
Double-sided tape
Glue gun
Washing-up bottle cap
Single-serving drinks bottle

download available

Hidden deep within the Magical Inkpot's velvety darkness are all the words of all the stories yet to be told. Take my advice though; such rare and bewitching devices are not easy to come by. Adventurers better than I have given over large fortunes and spent many a long expedition in search of pristine examples. I am certain that the same fate would have befallen me, had I not chanced up on a looseleaf portfolio, within whose faded clutches lay the clear and simple instructions for a Magical Inkpot's fabrication, which I hereby pass to you.

Granted, when using the magical ink, the pen does drape itself in a certain overly rich verbosity, that may on occasion get in the way of what one is actually trying to say ... by which I mean, that is, it easy to fall under the spell of the Magical Inkpot's delicately wrought charms ... but there is no denying it is a great place to keep your quill.

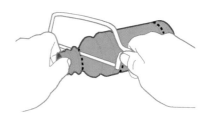

magical ink pot

1 You will need a small drink bottle and a squeezable sauce bottle cap, with or without flip over lid.

4 Cut the top of the bottle off. The plastic is hard here so use a hacksaw. Kids can use a junior hacksaw safely, and it's good practice, but you should steady the bottle.

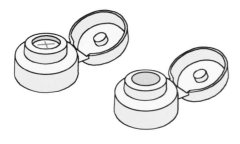

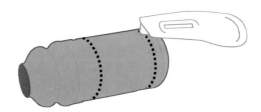

2 Remove the rubber insert valve.

5 Carefully cut the bottle to the other marks using either a craft knife or pair of strong kitchen scissors.

SPACE FOR LABEL

GLUE   GRAVEL

3 Mark round the bottle to cut off the top and most of the flat part of the middle, leaving some space for the label in the finished ink pot.

6 Tape the two halves of the bottle back together with sticky tape and half fill with some gravel and a bit of glue-gun glue to stop the stones rattling.

▶

GLUE

7 Carefully glue the cap in place by glueing the underside of the cap and spray the whole thing with black spray paint.

8 Cut out some paper to fit and stick it round the base using double-sided tape or a blob of glue-gun glue.

9 All your finished ink pot needs now is a magical quill and you are ready to write your first spell.

Go to our website to print this stylish label for your ink pot.

dragon hunter's goggles

At the height of the dragon-hunting boom, hardly a week went by without the London press running a story of some hapless adventurer, fried to a crisp in the blast of a super-heated roar. As you might imagine, a whole industry grew up selling specialised protective dragon-hunting equipment.

As a dragon hunter myself, there was one item that I would never have been without; my flare-resistant Glaremaster goggles. Extremely lightweight with ground sapphire lenses, these wonderful goggles offer a supreme level of ocular protection for the riskiest dragon encounters.

Even now, when there are no more dragons to vanquish, the goggles come in very handy. The company that originally made my Sapphire Glaremasters over 150 years ago is no longer in business, but don't let that trouble you, because now you can make a pair yourself. Collinworth has provided you with a set of excellent instructions and a template to assist you in your efforts.

Make your own flare-resistant Glaremaster dragon hunter's goggles

8 years +

90 minutes

Fabric or leather
2 x Poly-bottle caps
2l PET fizzy drink bottle
Gold paint (pen)
Transparent coloured cellophane sweet wrapper
Glue
Velcro

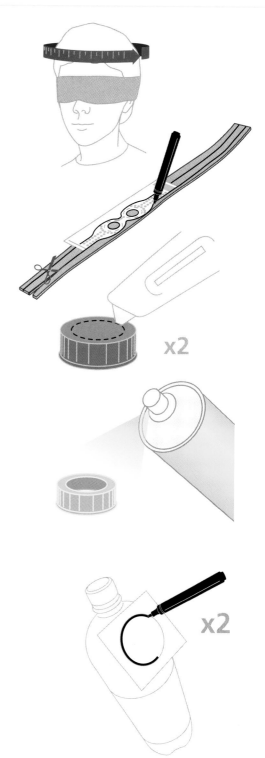

1. Measure round the head. You'll be surprised how big the measurement is. Ideally just wrap the thick fabric or preferably leather strip you are going to use round the head and mark off the length with a permanent marker. Remember to leave some overlap for the Velcro (hook and eye) fixing.

2. Cut out the shape of the goggles from the template sheet and lay it on the fabric or leather at the centre of the strip and draw round it with a marker. Then cut out the shape, including the eye holes, using a strong pair of scissors.

3. Cut most of the centre from two poly-bottle (milk bottle) closures so that you leave a small rim round the edge. Some closures have a rim inside which is useful to follow as a cutting guide. If your closures don't, then you'll need to draw a guideline round with a marker before you start cutting. Take care with sharp knives and only cut soft polythene plastic lids.

4. Paint both closures with gold paint. You can use spray, gold felt-tip markers or gold paint. Put them on one side to dry while you make the rest of the goggles.

5. Select the circle guide that best fits the bottle lid diameter that you have. Trace the template square and then carefully cut out the correct circle.

6. Use the circle template to draw two circles on the shoulder of a 2 litre drink bottle with a permanent marker.

circle guide TEMPLATE

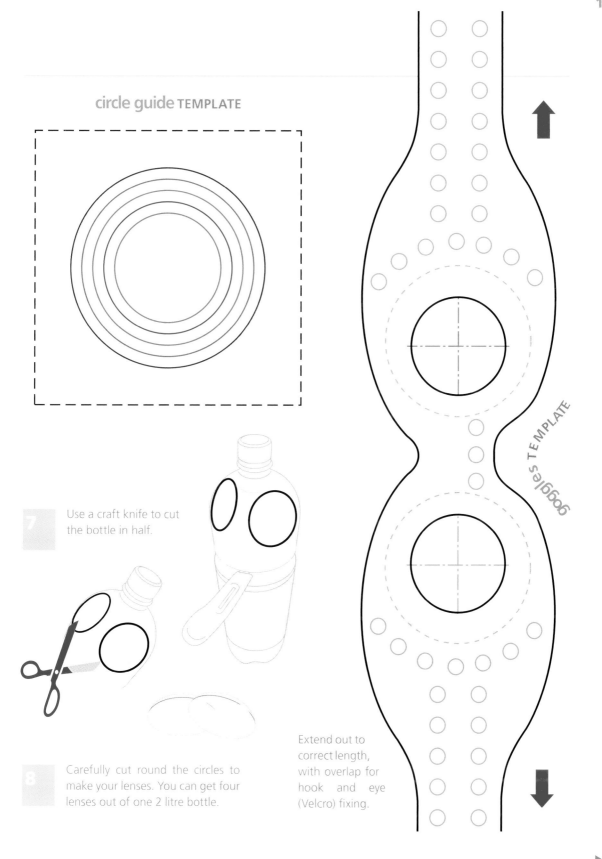

goggles TEMPLATE

7 Use a craft knife to cut the bottle in half.

8 Carefully cut round the circles to make your lenses. You can get four lenses out of one 2 litre bottle.

Extend out to correct length, with overlap for hook and eye (Velcro) fixing.

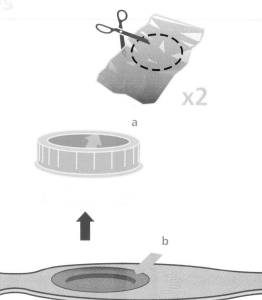

x2

a

9 To make the inner coloured filters, cut two circles of boiled sweet wrapper cellophane (or similar) about the same size as the lenses. Check out whether you can see through the sheet by holding it close to your eyes, most sweet wrappers and even some crisp bag metalised plastic foils are actually see-through if you look up close.

b

c

10 Assemble the eye pieces by first sticking the lens inside the golden ring. To do this, first put some glue inside the ring (**a**). If using glue-gun glue, wait a few seconds for it to cool slightly before pressing in the lens as the very hot glue can melt the lens slightly and spoil the look of it. Next put a ring of glue on the goggle strap just round the eye hole (**b**) and stick the colour filter film to that. Lastly apply some glue to the underside of the ring (**c**) and stick that to the goggle strip.

11 Using a gold or silver marker, or a paintbrush, make a number of small dots along the goggle strip as shown on the template. Alternatively make up your own pattern.

12 Don't forget the Velcro (hook and eye fastener). Use a self-adhesive version, and sew or stick with glue-gun glue. Remember that the Velcro is stuck to the front of one end and the back of the other end so that the strap lays flat when the Velcro is fastened.

Use a ski goggle or large glasses case to keep your Glaremasters safe and ready for use.

BIG KITCHEN SCIENCE

This experiment involves mixing salt with water, to make a saturated solution. It's a reasonably quick, fun experiment to do but the crystal growing takes days. This makes it perfect if your kids don't live with you, because they'll look forward to seeing the progress when they come to visit. The experiment can be used as a basis for some interesting discussions about crystals and solutions, which you can record in a results booklet, downloadable from our website.

Cultivate a big crystal using nothing more than salt and water

When growing your salt crystal, don't use dishwasher salt as this has various anti-caking additives in it which make it impossible for a big crystal to grow. Sugar also makes a fabulous crystal, but it does take much longer to form.

6 years +

1 hour (plus growing time)

Empty jam jar or drinking glass
Salt
Thread
Wire coathanger or small stick

download available

Pour half a mug of salt into 600ml of warm water. Do not use salt with added anticaking agents.

SALT

Stir until the salt is dissolved, keep adding a little salt and stirring until no more salt will dissolve.

Carefully pour the solution into a clean jam jar or glass making sure that you don't pour any salt in.

MAGNIFIED SALT
SEED CRYSTAL

Tie a piece of thread round the biggest salt crystal you can find in the unused salt you have.

Tie the thread round a piece of coathanger wire or drinking straw and dangle it in the solution.

Watch your salt crystal grow. But don't hold your breath, it grows slowly, very slowly.

Every couple of days lift the crystal out and pour the water into another jar, leaving behind the crystals that have grown on the bottom.

8 After about a week, your crystal should have grown. Take it out and dry it carefully on kitchen roll, then hang it up or put it in the booklet you can download from our website.

BIG KITCHEN SCIENCE

Experimental discussion

What is a salt crystal made of?

Trillions and trillions of sodium chloride molecules all arranged neatly in rows. As its name suggests, sodium chloride (the chemical name for salt) is made up of the two chemical elements, sodium and chlorine. The scientific way of writing this is NaCl (Na = Sodium, Cl = Chlorine). The molecules line up so that salt forms a cubic crystal.

How does the crystal grow?

As some water evaporates from the solution, the remaining water can't hold the salt in solution. The salt is deposited one molecule at a time and little crystals form. The salt molecules line themselves up in neat rows because that is the way they can fit together using the least amount of energy.

Why do we need salt?

Salt contains sodium, and sodium is a vital chemical used by the body to make nerves work and help regulate the body's water levels. However, too much is bad for us and causes high blood pressure.

How much salt is there in sea water?

There are 78 kg of salt for every cubic meter of sea water. However, salt only makes up about three-quarters of the minerals dissolved in sea water.

Help your kids be creative – part one

Children start out as naturally creative, and by helping them to develop their innate creativity you will enable them to be happier, perform better at school and be more successful as they grow up. Creativity is about so much more than drawing a pretty picture or making a great model. It is what helps your children develop the ability to see a problem from more than one angle. It helps them find new solutions by using the knowledge they already have as imaginatively as possible in a wide range of school subjects and real-life situations. Creativity will also help your children to negotiate by allowing them to see the other person's point of view. As they grow up, being creative will improve their school grades and eventually help them in their jobs and with all their relationships.

As a parent, you are in the perfect position to develop your children's creativity, and it is not something that you can just leave to their school to sort out. Despite the fact that the modern curriculum recognises that creativity is critical to a child's development, large classes are no match for the potential benefit of your undivided, one-to-one attention.

So, here are ten great ways to develop your child's creativity and help them fulfil their potential.

1 Fire up their imagination

Be creative when you talk to your children. Discuss with them the things you see together, whether that be television programmes, films or things that happen in your neighbourhood. Read to them. The best and probably easiest time for this is at bedtime. It is a great routine to get into and there are some fantastic books out there. When you read, try to bring the words to life by putting on accents for the different characters or reading slowly and expressively. That in itself is inventive and creative, and children don't mind if the accents are all wrong – they just love that they can imagine how the story is filled with different characters.

Tell your kids about anything interesting that you have done or seen since you last saw them, and describe the events in a way that paints a picture of the scene for them. Use descriptive words and where appropriate describe what you felt about the situation. Finally, take them on creative outings now and again, go to the zoo, a museum or an art gallery. It doesn't take much to get a kid's creativity and imagination going.

2 Answer their questions

Always try to answer your children's questions. Handled correctly and presented in a way that they can understand, children can take on board the concepts behind almost any subject, and answering their questions is a way of showing them that you approve of their inquisitiveness. Children are learning machines and are naturally very curious, so even if you don't know the answer to a question, look it up in a book or on the web.

That doesn't mean that your kids shouldn't have to think for themselves. Creativity is about batting ideas back and forth, thinking round a problem, challenging what you know and exploring the limits. If you think that they might already know the answer to their own question, then encourage them to say it. Ask them things like: "Why do you think that is?" or "What would be a better way of doing that?" or "Why do you think it works like that?". Be prepared to prompt them, but try to let them work some things out for themselves. It's quite likely that you will be surprised by how clear their thinking is and how much they really know.

3 Spend time with them to get them started

Kids need your time. They want to be with you and when they are spending time with you that they know isn't rushed, they can relax and let their creativity come to the fore. A great way (and perhaps the most obvious way) to develop your children's creativity is to make stuff with them. It could be anything from brick models to plastic construction kits to any other type of craft. When you start out making things together, it is likely that you will have to provide most of the impetus to get things going. Persevere, let them do as much as possible, and help them out where their lack of skill is clearly frustrating them. However, try not to end up doing the whole thing yourself while they idly look on, or worse still, go off and play the games console. If they do start to get bored, put the project away and get it out another day when they, and you, are fresh. From a creativity point of view, the process is just as important as the end result.

Don't be put off if what you make together isn't very good to start with. If you keep trying, the end results will get better and better as your child (and you) practise and improve.

4 Provide them with the kit

It's always said that a bad workman blames his tools, but there is nothing more frustrating than trying to do something with the wrong equipment. Depending on what you plan to do, make sure that you have a small making kit ready. Whether you are going to make something from this book or just invent something, then a few permanent marker felt pens, some rapid glue or a glue gun and a couple of cans of spray paint are all you'll really need for most projects.

Creativity doesn't have to be limited to doing specific 'creative' projects. When you go out, if you are going to be in the car or on the train, take a pad and one or two pencils with you. A small amount of kit like this not only makes any journey much easier but also can provide a really nice extra dimension to the day out itself when you stop to draw one of the animals at the zoo, or something you've seen in the park.

5 Provide them with the opportunity

Sometimes you might have to turn off the television and the computer console and get all the making stuff out to get your kids started. You could:

- Have a painting and doing afternoon – On a sunny afternoon get a roll of blank lining wallpaper, unroll as much as possible on your garden fence and let the kids paint it with washable poster paints, making as much mess as they like
- Play creative games like Pictionary, or card games where there is an element of negotiation and decision-making, Pit, for example
- Learn how to play classic card games like Canasta, Bridge or Whist.

All these games and types of activity require creativity and original ways of problem-solving, and although some of the games can take time to learn they are very satisfying to play well.

*My father gave me
the greatest gift
anyone could give
another person, he
believed in me.*

JAMES (JIMMY V) VALVANO
Basketball coach

spaceship PAGE 167

MAKE A HYDROMETER

being there

HELP YOUR KIDS BE CREATIVE – PART TWO

ray gun PAGE 171

space rocket

Make a rocket ship from old packaging you have lying around

8 years +

1 hour

Glue gun
Marker
Craft knife
Crisps tube
Single-serving drink
bottle
Yoghurt carton
Toilet paper roll
Shaving foam cap
Cardboard
Paper

You don't have to be a rocket scientist to make a rocket from junk packaging. These instructions show you how to do it with a crisps tube and a toilet paper tube, but any collection of tubes will do. Cut off a single-serving drink bottle top for the engine nozzle and a deodorant spray cap for the nose cone and the rest is easy.

For our rocket, I didn't stick the crisps tube lid down – that meant we could take it apart and later we made a simple satellite to go inside so that when 'in space' the satellite could be deployed.

Here are some tips:
1. Cover the tubes in white A4 paper before you glue them together so that you can draw on them easily; this saves you having to paint them.

2. Draw your graphics and some black lines and boxes on to the paper before you wrap it round the tubes; it's much easier to draw on flat paper!

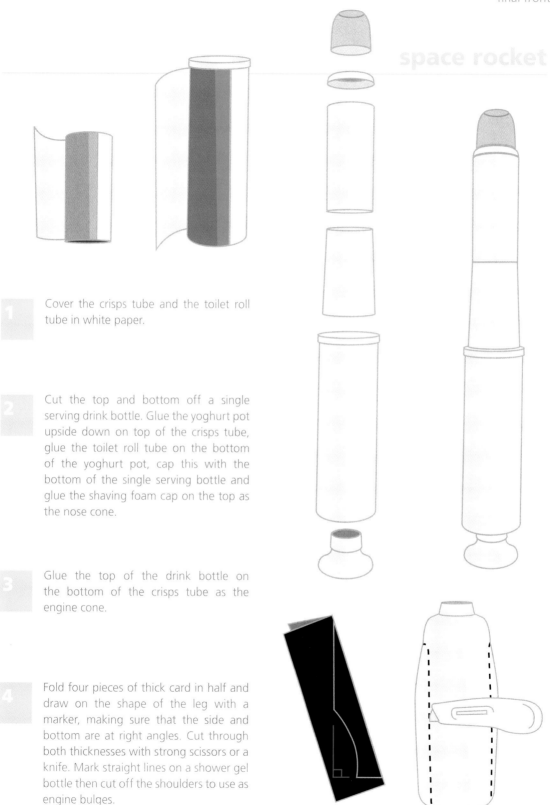

space rocket

1 Cover the crisps tube and the toilet roll tube in white paper.

2 Cut the top and bottom off a single serving drink bottle. Glue the yoghurt pot upside down on top of the crisps tube, glue the toilet roll tube on the bottom of the yoghurt pot, cap this with the bottom of the single serving bottle and glue the shaving foam cap on the top as the nose cone.

3 Glue the top of the drink bottle on the bottom of the crisps tube as the engine cone.

4 Fold four pieces of thick card in half and draw on the shape of the leg with a marker, making sure that the side and bottom are at right angles. Cut through both thicknesses with strong scissors or a knife. Mark straight lines on a shower gel bottle then cut off the shoulders to use as engine bulges.

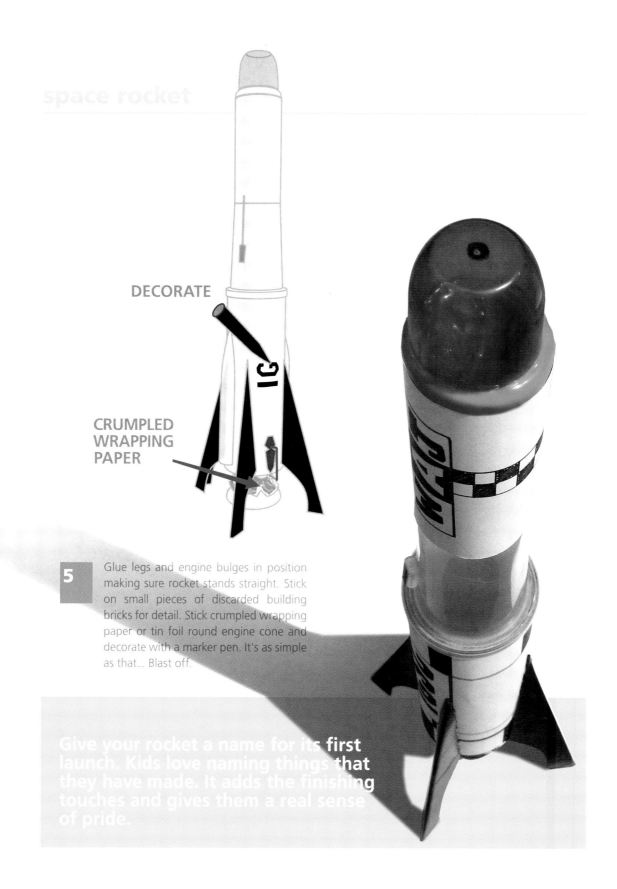

DECORATE

CRUMPLED
WRAPPING
PAPER

5 Glue legs and engine bulges in position making sure rocket stands straight. Stick on small pieces of discarded building bricks for detail. Stick crumpled wrapping paper or tin foil round engine cone and decorate with a marker pen. It's as simple as that... Blast off.

Give your rocket a name for its first launch. Kids love naming things that they have made. It adds the finishing touches and gives them a real sense of pride.

spaceship

This is such an easy and pleasing project and has given my children hours of fun. As the washing-up liquid bottle (the canopy part) was made of clear plastic, we sprayed the inside of that black before sticking it to the body to make it look really shiny when finished. Just remember to mask off the window part before spraying the rest of the body colour. Once the red, or any other body colour you like, has been sprayed, you can use artists' acrylic paints to finish it off. Use a wash of black to make certain parts look old, worn out or dirty, and paint contrasting colours as lines and rings in certain places to add detail. You can also add alien-looking numbers or letters.

Trace over the special wing template provided. For our wings we used foamboard, but any thick or corrugated cardboardwould be just as good for the job.

Make this incredible spaceship and look like a professional model maker

12 years +

1 hour
(incl. glue drying)

Craft knife
Glue gun
Marker
Hacksaw
Shower gel bottle
Washing-up liquid
   bottle
2 x Toothbrushes
2 x Felt-tip pens
Cardboard

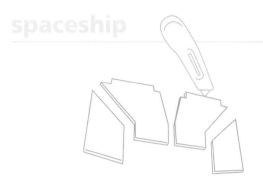

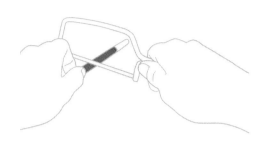

1 Trace over the wing template, stick it on to some thick card and carefully cut it out using a craft knife. **Take care with sharp knives, do not let children use them without help. Use strong scissors where possible.**

2 Offer the cut out wing up to the side of the shower gel bottle and mark off a slot for the wing tab. (Use the seam of the bottle as a guide). Cut out the hole with a craft knife.

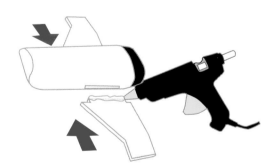

3 Use glue-gun glue or very rapid epoxy resin to glue the wings to the shower gel bottle, pushing the wing tab fully into the slot you cut in the side of the bottle. **Note: the wings are swept forward.**

4 Using a hacksaw or serrated knife cut the two old felt-tip pens down in size so that they just fit over the wings.

Also cut the handle ends off two old toothbrushes.

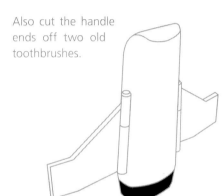

5 Glue the caps on the felt pens and then stick the cut off felt pens against the fuselage on the top of each wing.

6 Stick the wing thickener on top of the wing, pushed up against the felt pen barrel.

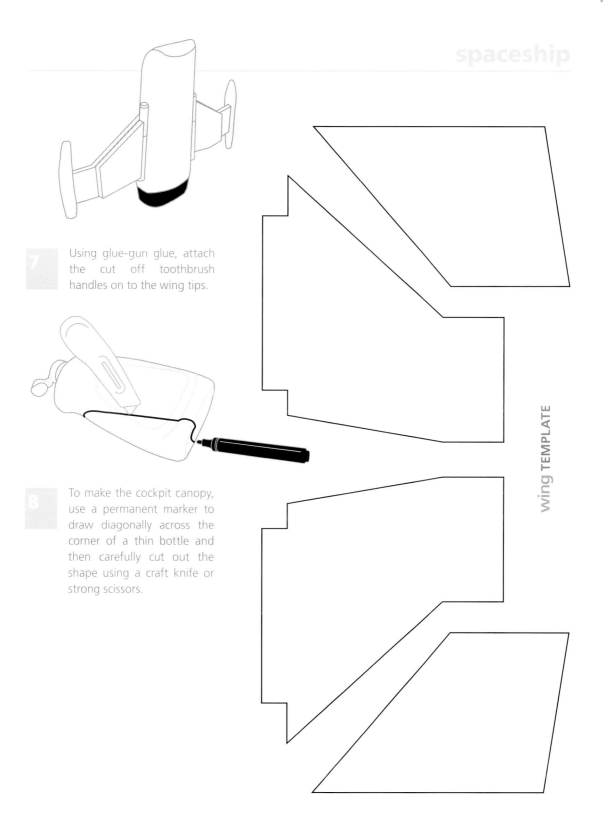

7 Using glue-gun glue, attach the cut off toothbrush handles on to the wing tips.

8 To make the cockpit canopy, use a permanent marker to draw diagonally across the corner of a thin bottle and then carefully cut out the shape using a craft knife or strong scissors.

wing **TEMPLATE**

11 Push canopy down on to glue ring.

9 Offer the canopy to the fuselage (but do **not** glue it yet) and marker round it.

12 Paint the spaceship according to your own colour scheme.

10 Glue-gun glue is too hot for the thin bottle when it comes out of the gun, so put glue on to the fuselage and wait 10–15 seconds before pushing the canopy into place.

If you use corrugated card you could seal up the edge of the wing with glue-gun glue to give a better finish.

ray gun

My sons thought up some inventive equipment inspired by the games they like best – hand-held arms that shoot whirlwinds, suck up water, or even turn things into chickens. Having looked at what junk we had in the 'making box', we decided to make this ray gun, called a pulse rifle, which shoots out a laser ray with rings of light surrounding it.

It's not that hard to put together, but the skill is in making it so that it looks like a pulse rifle, and if you get the grip size right it feels great in the hand. Once we had finished making it, the kids even abandoned the virtual game for a while in favour of acting out the story themselves.

Get your kids up out of their chairs

10 years +

90 minutes

Detergent bottle
Sport drink bottle
Single serving drink bottle
Pieces of aluminium foil
Glue gun
Drinking cup
Thick cardboard
Spray paint

1 To make the stock, either use a thin, wide short bottle or make your own by cutting down a thin washing detergent bottle as shown. Carefully mark round the bottle horizontally and then cut the bottle with a pair of strong scissors. Check the size of the bottle where you mark so that one end fits neatly inside the other.

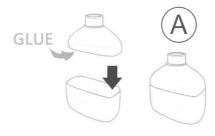

GLUE

(A)

2 For the best effect, use glue-gun glue and apply to the rim that fits inside the other and then push the two parts of the bottle together making sure that they are straight.

(B)

3 Mark and then cut about two-thirds off a plastic disposable cup to make the muzzle end.

4 The barrel is made in two parts. A straight metallic part and a larger shaped part. The straight part is simply made by wrapping a piece of tin foil round a toilet paper tube. Thicker foil is better, so used takeaway food trays are ideal, but any kitchen foil will do. The second, shaped part of the barrel is made from an old sports drink bottle (see assembly, step 13).

(C)

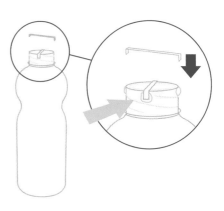

5 The telescopic sight makes this model really fun to play with. The sight is made from any small single serving drinks bottle. Glue thin strips of foil in the shape of a cross over the open neck of the bottle.

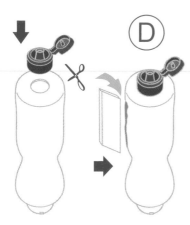

ray gun

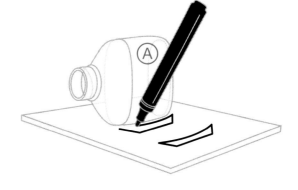

6 Cut a hole in the base of the bottle and glue-gun glue a lid from a washing up detergent bottle over it. The live-hinged cap lid is now the sight scope cover. If you put your eye up to the small hole, you can see the cross hairs clearly at the other end. Cut a small parallelogram-shaped piece of thick cardboard for the site mount and glue it to the side of the bottle.

8 Wrap the grip block in paper, lightweight card or thick aluminium foil. Trim off the wrapping to the edge of the thick cardboard block.

x4

7 Make the grip using the template provided. Mark out and cut four long, thin, identically sized, parallelogram-shaped pieces of thick cardboard and glue them together to make a single block.

9 Although glue-gun glue is strong, the top of the grip will see a lot of stress during play, so cut two strengthening plates from thick card. To make sure that they will fit the shape of the stock, draw round its profile with a marker.

grip TEMPLATE

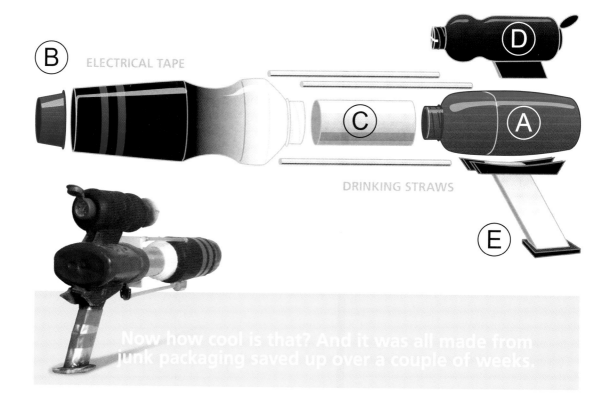

10 Glue the support plates either side of the grip so that the top of the plates line up with the cut top of the grip block.

11 Cut out a square of thick cardboard slightly bigger than the end of the grip and glue to the end of the grip.

12 For a neat finish, paint each part before assembling the Ray Gun. Choose whatever colours you like. Ray guns always seem to be brightly coloured, especially in your favourite games console game.

13 Assemble the parts as shown.

14 Decorate the Ray Gun with electrical tape, and glue drinking straws (sprayed silver) between the stock and the expansion barrel. Add extra finishing touches using whatever you have to hand: wires, springs or little bits of circuit board. In fact anything vaguely technical-looking will add great detail.

B ELECTRICAL TAPE

DRINKING STRAWS

Now how cool is that? And it was all made from junk packaging saved up over a couple of weeks.

satellite

For thousands of years humans have gazed up into the velvety blanket of the night sky in wonder. In 1995, the Hubble Space Telescope stared deep into space for ten days and built up an image of what it could see stretching right to the edge of the visible universe. The image it showed us is mind-blowing. In an area of sky that is only the size of the eye of a needle held at arm's length, the Hubble imaged at least 1,500 galaxies. Given that each galaxy has around 500 billion stars in it, in just that one tiny portion of the night sky, the Hubble was looking at a mind-boggling 750 trillion stars. Now with that thought running through your head, go and make a model of the Hubble Space Telescope to remind yourself how amazing the universe really is.

Make your own model satellite, just like the Hubble Space Telescope

10 years +

90 minutes

2 x Toilet paper
 tubes
Kitchen foil
Paper clips
Sieve mesh
Craft knife
Glue-gun glue
Marker
Gold paint
Cardboard

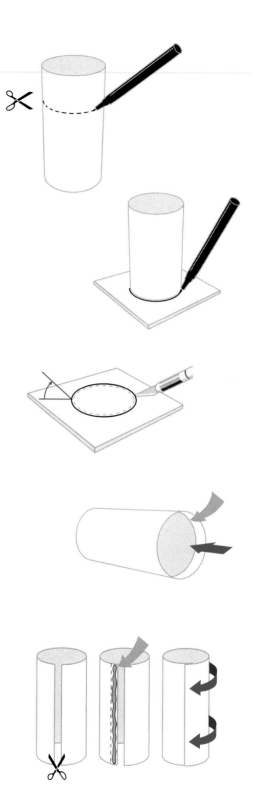

1 Mark a horizontal line about two thirds of the way along a toilet paper tube and then neatly cut round the line.

2 Carefully mark round the tube (making sure that you don't squeeze it into an oval shape) to make a circle the same size as the tube on a thick piece of corrugated cardboard or foamboard.

3 Carefully cut out the circle just inside the line. If you make the cut at a slight angle, it will really help you in the next stage, when you have to fit the cardboard circle inside the toilet tube end.

4 The base is recessed. Check that the circle fits before you add the glue, if it is too big, mark where it doesn't fit, and trim it to fit. For a neat finish, when glueing, put the glue inside the end of the tube and push the cardboard circle into the tube. This keeps the outside of the tube neat and free of glue and the circle wipes the glue down inside the tube. Put this to one side and now make the second tube.

5 The satellite telescope is made of two concentric tubes (much like an old fashioned hand-held ship's telescope), so the second tube needs to fit inside the first one. The thinner tube is longer than the one you have just prepared, so it doesn't need to be cut shorter. Instead, make a vertical cut in the second tube and glue it back together so that the cut edges overlap and it has a smaller diameter.

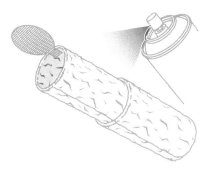

6 Check that the new thinner tube ,fits inside the first one you made. It does not have to be a tight fit. Cover both tubes in slightly crumpled aluminium kitchen foil. This is easily done by rolling the foil round the tubes and then tucking the ends over. Stick it to the tubes using glue-gun glue, or double sided sticky tape for a quick result.

9 Spray the entire assembly with gold paint. If you don't have gold paint, use white or leave the original silver of the aluminium foil. Spray the lid end first, as the lid is made of cardboard it will dry quickly. As soon as the lid is dry, you can hold the assembly by the edge of the lid and spray the rest without ending up with gold fingers.

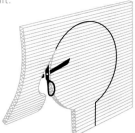

7 To make the telescope lid cut a small, table-tennis-bat shaped piece of thin corrugated card, so that the circle is about the same diameter as that of the thinner of the two tubes.

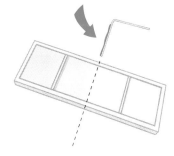

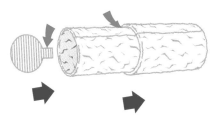

8 Glue the thinner tube inside the thicker one. For a neat result put the glue inside the thicker tube and push the thinner tube on to the glue. You only need to push the thinner tube about 1cm in. Make sure that the foil seams line up. Glue the telescope lid into the inside of the open end of the thinner tube with its handle on the opposite side to the seams.

10 To make the solar cells, cut out two rectangles of thin corrugated cardboard about as wide as the tube and nearly as long as the telescope. Stick two slightly smaller rectangles of holographic wrapping paper (or similar) on to the panels (one on each side). Bend a paper clip at right angles and glue into the thickness of the cardboard. Use paperclips to make other surface details or to break up the panel into smaller sub panels.

▶

11 To make the satellite communications dish carefully straighten and then bend a large paper clip as shown.

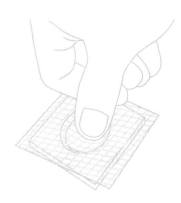

14 To make the satellite dish, ideally you should use a soft metal mesh of the type used in auto-body repair. It can be bought at most car spares shops in small sheets. It is low cost and cuts and deforms easily. If you can't get hold of that, use a small piece of tea-strainer or sieve mesh, or failing that, a piece of aluminium foil.

12 Mark round the shape on to a piece of thick cardboard.

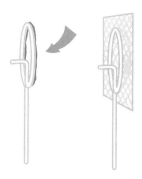

13 Carefully cut a hole out of the cardboard, at a slight angle if possible. You are going to be using this as the former for a small bit of mesh, so an angled cut will help you get a satellite dish-shaped mesh.

15 Apply a ring of glue-gun glue to the round part of the satellite frame and glue the mesh on to it so that the ring of the frame lines up with the indent you have made in the mesh.

satellite

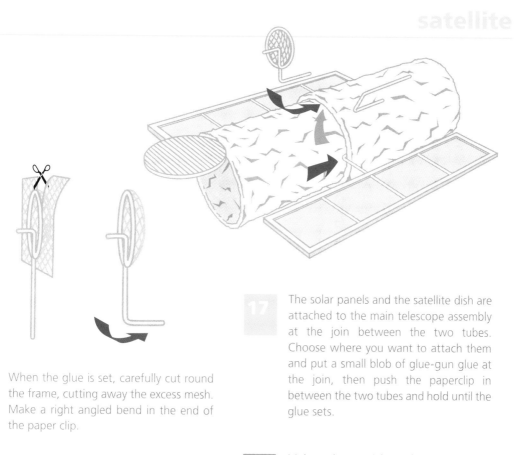

16 When the glue is set, carefully cut round the frame, cutting away the excess mesh. Make a right angled bend in the end of the paper clip.

17 The solar panels and the satellite dish are attached to the main telescope assembly at the join between the two tubes. Choose where you want to attach them and put a small blob of glue-gun glue at the join, then push the paperclip in between the two tubes and hold until the glue sets.

18 Make other aerials and more satellite dishes if you want and attach them in the same way.

The real Hubble Space Telescope is the size of a small truck and weighs in at over 11 tonnes.

Test the density of liquids with this simple-to-make hydrometer

The world is an interesting place, and you are one of the best people to show your children just how fascinating it is. On p182 there are a few key facts about the experiment, designed to help you engage your children's interest and explain in simple terms what's going on in the experiment.

6 years +

20 minutes

Cheap ballpoint pen
Drinking glass
Blu-Tack
Glue gun (optional)

download available

This experiment involves mixing water with salt or sugar, and seeing the difference it makes to the thickness (mass or specific gravity) of water by measuring it with a homemade hydrometer. Once made, the hydrometer can be used to measure the relative specific gravity of a range of water-based fluids and drinks. The experiment can be used as a basis for some interesting discussions about solvents and solutes and how things dissolve and will reinforce subjects your kids will be learning at school at some point. Go to our website to print a neat little fold-up book which can be filled in, and is something nice to keep as a record of the experiment you did together.

1. Take one cheap ballpoint pen.

2. Remove the nib and ink reservoir.

3. Plug one end with a little glue-gun glue.

4. Push a blob of Blu-Tack on the same end.

5. Fill a large glass with water and slowly lower the hydrometer into the water.

6. Adjust the weight of the hydrometer by adding or removing some blu tack until it floats as low as possible in the water.

7. Carefully mark the water level on the hydrometer with a permanent marker.

8. Mix up some different solutions (i.e. using salt or sugar) and float the hydrometer in each of them and mark each to see the difference.

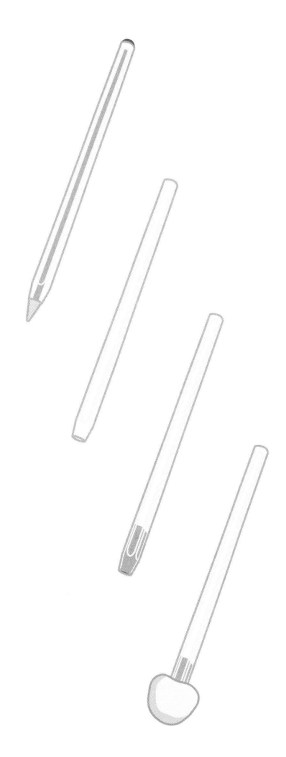

Why does the hydrometer float, given that it is open at the top?

The fluid it displaces weighs less for the same volume (has less mass) than the hydrometer.

Why does the sugar and or salt (solute) dissolve in the water (solvent)?

The sugar or salt molecules are broken off by the water and mingle with the water molecules. Note: This is a physical reaction and is therefore reversible. You can make it go back so that you have sugar and water separated again.

Why does the hydrometer float at different levels in the different solutions?

The solutions are denser than water, thus weigh more per volume (mass) and so the mass of the hydrometer displaces less of their volume and as a result floats higher.

How is a hydrometer used in the real world?

Manufacturers of beer use a hydrometer to check how much alcohol is dissolved in their beers.

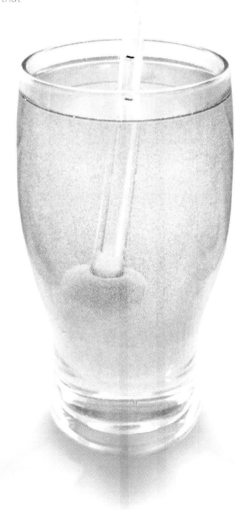

BEING THERE

Help your kids be creative – part two

6 Plan your creative time

When you start out on a making project, have a clear idea of what you want to make and roughly how you are going to make it. Whether you follow an existing plan or make one of your own, preparation is an essential part of doing any project. Usually kids (and most likely you) will want to dive straight in and start sticking things together, but while this is great instant fun it is not developing your creativity. Working out how to solve problems and chatting through the best ways of putting items together, colours for paint and the order to do things in, will give your kids invaluable experience at problem solving.

At school your children will have been taught that the most important part of any project is the plan, but often they see this as the boring part of the project, where nothing is getting done. However, if you can make the planning quick and fun, it is potentially one of the most inventive times, the moment when all things are possible and you can fantasise about how fabulous the finished thing will be. Why not:

- Get your children to look for junk packaging and any materials and equipment you are going to need
- With your kids, draw some quick sketches of the finished item, showing which bits go where
- Discuss any problems that you think you might encounter and work out how you are going to get round them. This may involve trying out to see how things go together before you stick them together permanently.

7 Do creative things that the children like

Although one aspect of creativity is complete freedom of expression, by far the most useful application of creativity is to solve problems and make things the way you want them. Creative activities with your children will be much more fun if they relate to something that the kids really like already and for which they need something that you can make together. You could design and make:

- A game card display book
- A football league or score chart
- A prop from a recent movie
- Something from one of their console games

Kids love to make their games real by role-playing their way through stories and scenes that they have seen on television, at the cinema or on their console games. They will be amazed to find out that with your help they can make items and props from their favourite stories that will allow them to translate the game into their real life role-play versions. Things you make together are likely to be much more fun and more played with than shop-bought merchandise, as well as being a whole lot cheaper.

helicopter PAGE 105

▶

Don't rush them

While there should be an emphasis on completing tasks, doing something creatively is not a race. Children participate in so many activities that are geared towards winning that it is hard for them to understand that getting something done and solving problems, so that the end result is what they want, is better than finishing first.

In our society we are obsessed with the need to instil a desire to win in our children. In most cases this only results in turning out grown-ups who at some level are disappointed with themselves and their lives. Developing creativity is not in itself about winning. In the long run, approaching life creatively will make you more successful and happier, but when doing projects with your children, don't make them rush to false deadlines. You can always put the stuff away and get it out next time, or if they want, finish it for them when they are not there, so that it's done when you next see them.

Don't use false praise

When you are pleased that your child is doing something creative and you want to encourage them, it is very hard not to tell them how brilliant what they are doing is – even when it is clearly not. Children are very perceptive to emotions and know when someone is saying something that they don't really mean. On the other hand children need to feel that you approve of them and that you are proud of them. As a parent, it's very difficult to judge how good something that your child has done really is because you have very little to compare it with. If you do a lot of craft with your children, you get to know when they are doing something that is very good and something of which they are proud, and then you can tell them that it is amazing. As you work

together with your children you will also develop a way of discussing the things that you do that it not judgemental, where you can assess the quality of the outcome together.

However, to start with, consider what they are doing in terms of their age and the amount of experience or practice they have had at it. If things don't turn out exactly as planned and could do with improvement, use comments like "That's great for a first try" or "I think that that is very good for someone your age", which are much better than any false flattery. Ask your child which bit they liked doing the most and which bit they didn't like doing. Ask them how they could improve it if they had another go at it. During the project, if you see things going wrong, helping them with what's causing a problem will go a long way towards improving the final outcome. Don't wrestle the tools or project off them though, or they will feel that it has started to become your project and not theirs. Offer to help. Ask them "What can I do to help?", "Do you need me to hold something?", "Do you need some help spraying because the button is too hard to press?" Remember, the act of making something is at least as important as the outcome.

Don't be negative about their ideas

Developing your children's creativity is about showing them how to have more ideas and giving them the skill to choose the best ones to improve the outcome. There are a few classic techniques for generating and developing ideas and lines of thinking and none of them rely on negative comments. Negative comments stifle creativity. They inhibit the free flow of ideas from one person to another, because being in an atmosphere of negative comments makes most people think twice about putting their ideas forward. When this happens, vital ideas are lost and only the most insensitive individuals or those with the loudest voices get heard. To develop your children's creativity, listen to their ideas. If you feel that they are stuck in a rut thinking about a solution that is not right, then help them build on it and develop it, and encourage them to think round the problem from an alternative viewpoint.

If you would like to make more of the idea-generating process, then you might like to try the classic brainstorming technique of writing the ideas on sticky notes and putting them on a wall. Use a big marker to write with so that only the core nugget of each idea can be captured. Write one idea per sticky note and try to break down the ideas in to their most basic elements. These might be multiple answers to such

questions as, "What would be the best glue to use?", or "What should we use for the main body of the model?", or "Does it need to float?". As the ideas start to flow, the sticky notes can be moved about, enabling you to group the ideas together with other similar ideas into themes. By doing this you can see if there are areas that you have missed. When you do this with your kids, remember to keep your role as facilitator, adding ideas only to spark off new areas to consider and encouraging your children to consider the problem rigorously.

fluffy ladybird PAGE 37

*A father is someone that
holds your hand at the fair
makes sure you do what your mother says
holds back your hair when you are sick
brushes that hair when it is tangled
   because mother is too busy
lets you eat ice cream for breakfast
but only when mother is away
he walks you down the aisle
and tells you everything's gonna be ok.*

UNKNOWN

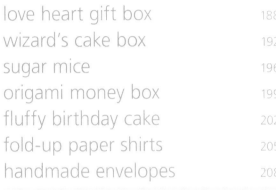

MÖBIUS STRIPS

being there
MAKE THE MOST OF A HOLIDAY

214

love heart gift box

Give a present to someone you love in this gorgeous handmade heart-shaped box

8 years +

2 hours (plus drying)

Cardboard
Newspaper
White glue
Paint

This lovely little project will show you how to make a papier-mâché box, just like the ones that you can buy in the shops. Getting the lid to fit is a piece of cake and the end result is the perfect way to wrap even the most expensive present.

We've painted ours on the outside with bright red acrylic paint, it covers the papier-mâché perfectly and can then be easily varnished with paint or spray to give a glossy finish. Paint the inside with a contrasting colour for a really nice effect. Fill the little box with pink tissue, torn and crumpled paper shreds or, like we have, with teased-out cotton wool balls. That way, whatever present you put inside will be kept safe, as well as looking beautiful when the box is opened. Choose one of the different sized love-heart templates and trace over it to make your box.

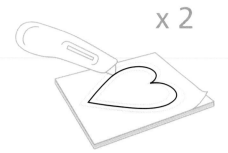

x 2

1 Trace over the template page and stick it to a piece of thick cardboard, select the size of heart you want and cut out. Draw round the cut out on to another piece of card and cut out a second heart exactly the same size. Make sure your cuts are vertical.

4 Glue the second strip of card round the double heart shape making sure that it lines up and does not overhang the edge. When set, carefully trim off any excess card that overhangs.

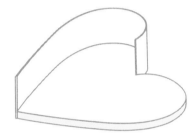

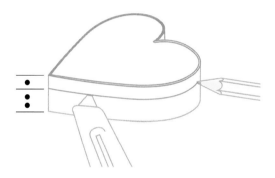

2 Trace the template measure and use it to cut two strips of card for as wide as the depth of the box you want and glue vertically round one half of one of the heart shapes (glue-gun glue is the best and quickest way to do this). Pre-bending the card by pulling it over the edge of a table top helps get the curve right.

5 Pencil mark a line round the box, so that the box is divided one third / two thirds and then, using a sharp craft knife, cut the box through all the way round at the line.

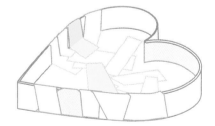

3 Glue the second heart shape to the top edge of the thin card so that the two heart shapes are parallel and square to the thin card upright section.

6 Tear small strips of newspaper and using white glue, cover the whole of both halves of the box (top and base) so that no part of the card is visible.

love heart gift box

box tray TEMPLATES

depth measure guide TEMPLATE

FOLD

FOLD

x 2

7 Cut two strips of thin card about 5mm to 10mm wider than the depth of the box bottom tray.

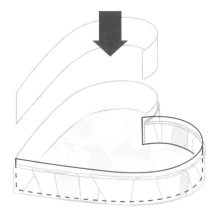

9 Paint the lid and base bright red, paint designs on the box, and/or paint the inside a contrasting colour. Gloss varnish the outside and fill with cotton wool and your gift.

8 Glue into the bottom tray so that the card pokes up above the edge of the tray by less than the depth of the top tray inside depth.

This gift box makes the perfect Valentine's present – either on its own or filled with something beautiful.

wizard's cake box

Create your own special box for cakes and sweets

12 years +

10 minutes

A4 paper
Stapler (optional)

download available

It was the success of Honeydukes, Hogsmeade's most famous sweet shop, which led three brothers to set up their own magical treat and cake shops. They baked and made all manner of delicious things and came to be known for their excellence throughout the wizarding world. Each shop had its own distinctive box, but being brothers, they followed each other's designs.

Now, for the first time, you can make these boxes simply and quickly from a single sheet of A4 thick paper or light card. Follow the template and cut the box out as accurately as you can, paying particular attention to the folding, because it is that which gives the box its neat appearance and shape. Gorgeous cake box graphic printables are available on our website.

Use these boxes to pack and keep your small cakes, sweets and treats just like a wizard, or give them as a lovely gift for that special person.

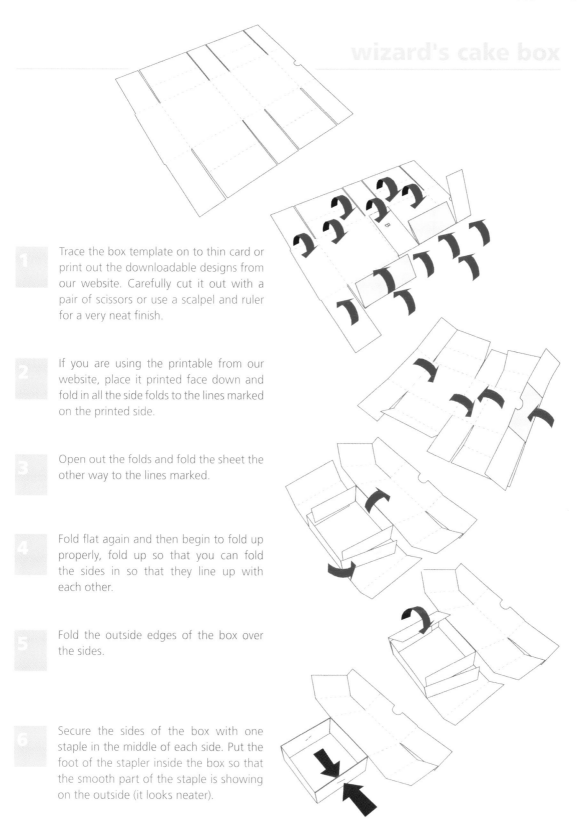

1. Trace the box template on to thin card or print out the downloadable designs from our website. Carefully cut it out with a pair of scissors or use a scalpel and ruler for a very neat finish.

2. If you are using the printable from our website, place it printed face down and fold in all the side folds to the lines marked on the printed side.

3. Open out the folds and fold the sheet the other way to the lines marked.

4. Fold flat again and then begin to fold up properly, fold up so that you can fold the sides in so that they line up with each other.

5. Fold the outside edges of the box over the sides.

6. Secure the sides of the box with one staple in the middle of each side. Put the foot of the stapler inside the box so that the smooth part of the staple is showing on the outside (it looks neater).

cake box TEMPLATE

wizard's cake box

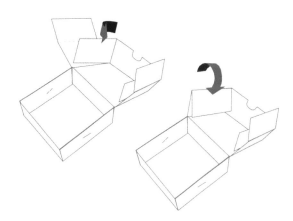

7 Fold in the top side flaps and then fold the top sides over, crease the edge well and you shouldn't need glue. They stay in place when the box is closed.

Wondering what to put inside? Just turn the page for some delicious treats.

sugar mice

Make these cute little sugar mice and then gobble them all up!

7 years +

40 minutes

2 x Mixing bowls or jugs
500g Icing sugar
1 Egg (medium)
Lemon juice
10ml Peppermint essence (optional)
10ml Water
Sugar laces

Sugar mice are wonderfully easy to make. No cooking is required, and provided you are careful with the amount of water or liquid you add (you only need a tiny amount) you should have very little trouble making some lovely little mice at your first attempt. For this recipe I have used sugar laces for the tails and added some ready mixed chocolate fudge detail icing. This is great for kids to use, it comes in handy little tubes in a range of colours and is really fun to apply as the finishing touch. Don't worry if your kids' mice are all misshapen and have odd eyes, the fun is in the making and then later – the eating. You don't need to add the lemon juice or traditional peppermint essence, so all you really need is some icing sugar and an egg and you're off and running.

sugar mice

1. Separate an egg so that you have only the white of one egg in a mixing bowl. To do this you crack and open the egg shell and tip the yolk back and forth between the two halves of the shell, letting the white dribble out.

2. Lightly whisk up the egg white so that it is a little bit frothy. If you have it, add a few drops of lemon juice, or if you want your mice to have a peppermint taste, then add a couple of drops of peppermint essence, although neither of these are necessary.

3. Pour three quarters of the contents of a packet of icing sugar into another mixing bowl. You will probably be able to make about ten mice with this. It's a good idea to save some icing sugar so that you have some to add to the mixture later if it gets too wet.

4. I can't stress how little water you need to add to the icing sugar in order to make the icing dough. Add the egg white mix a drop at a time and mix it into the icing sugar. You are aiming for a thick, solid but pliable dough. If your egg white isn't enough you can add a few drops of water at the end.

5. When the icing dough is solid and pliable, take it out of the bowl and roll it on a clean dry surface that you have lightly dusted with icing sugar. The dough should be firm enough to keep its shape if you roll it into a big ball. If it is still a bit runny, put it back in the bowl and add some more icing sugar.

▶

6 When you have got the dough to a firm, stable consistency, pinch off a small amount about the size of a large marble and roll it into a ball between the palms of your hands. Make sure your hands are clean and dry.

7 Make simple, smooth mouse shapes from each ball by gently pinching the sides of one end to make the nose. An ideal shape is a teardrop which has been flattened on the base. Do not make your mice too big, because they will take a long time to set and it is likely that they will slump as they set. Plus it will be too much to eat in one go!

8 The tails are made from confectionary sugar laces. Make a hole in the back of the mouse using a cocktail stick or a thin chopstick and poke the sugar lace in as far as possible, carefully smoothing the hole round the lace once it is poked right in.

9 The eyes are the finishing touch. To make them, first make one hole in each side of the head end with a cocktail stick, then either drop a tiny bead of melted chocolate into the hole or use shop-bought, pre-prepared chocolate fudge icing, dispensed conveniently from a small tube.

Eeny, meeny, miny, moe ...

origami money box

The word origami comes from a combination of the Japanese words *oru* meaning 'folding', and *gami* meaning 'paper'. Traditionally, origami requires the starting paper to be cut into a perfect square, but this creation uses rectangular paper – so, what better starting point for an origami model than the original 'folding stuff' – money?

The simple folds needed to make this lovely little open box can be learned in a few minutes. Crisp, new banknotes make beautifully detailed boxes, and as there is no tearing involved, the money can be easily unfolded and spent; double the fun. If you're giving money as a gift, why not make it more inventive by using two different-sized banknotes to form a closing box, with one box fitting inside the other, then very carefully wrap it up – neat.

Transform a banknote with this great party trick

7 years +

5 minutes

Rectangular piece of paper or banknote

origami money box

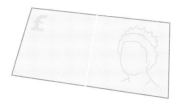

1 Take one small rectangular piece of paper, such as a banknote, bus ticket or till receipt.

6 Repeat for the other side, so that the concertina folds meet neatly in the middle.

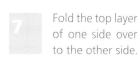

2 Fold in half lengthways.

7 Fold the top layer of one side over to the other side.

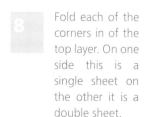

3 Unfold and lay flat.

8 Fold each of the corners in of the top layer. On one side this is a single sheet on the other it is a double sheet.

4 Fold two thirds of one side over.

9 Fold back the single layer.

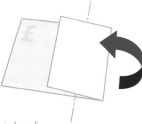

5 Fold that half back so that one side is concertina folded as far as the centre line.

10 Now you have to repeat the whole process for the other side. Fold over the top layer.

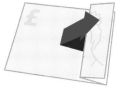

origami money box

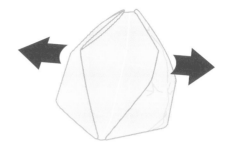

11 Turn the corners over so they neatly meet in the middle.

13 Pull apart the box so that it opens up.

12 Fold back the single layer so that you have a hexagonal piece of paper.

14 Shape the box at the corners by pinching the paper into nice neat creases.

A brilliant way to leave a tip in a restaurant!

fluffy birthday cake

This cute little cake makes an original birthday present

6 years+

1 hour

Cream wool
Red wool
Paper
String
Party candle holder

download available

What could be more creative and fun than a pompom in the shape of a birthday cake? This is great for your kids to make as a gift, and, if you're brave enough, it also makes a fantastic party game.

Two colours of wool are needed for the birthday cake pompom, although you could always make the jam filling using felt or material, or spray paint on to the wool through a mask. Either way you just need to choose two suitable colours. If you are feeling really inspired, why not try icing the cake with glue-gun glue, for a surreal look? Use the least amount of jam-coloured wool possible, as otherwise your jam layer will be too thick. As with the spooky flowers and fluffy ladybird projects, this pompom can be made with plastic bags instead of wool, so you can get going on this cake right away!

fluffy birthday cake

1. Trace the pompom disc template on p40 on to a thin piece of card and cut out two discs.

2. Prepare the wool by doubling it up so that you have pieces about 2m long in bundles of about six to ten strands, depending on how thick the wool is. You may need three or four such bundles.

3. Pass the wool through the hole in the middle of the disc repeatedly so that you wind it round the disc. Start with a red bundle making sure that the red wool thinly covers the entire disc. This is the jam layer and you don't want it too thick.

4. When the red has covered the disc, cut the waste off and start with the cake coloured bundle. Pass that through the disc hole repeatedly until you can't pass any more wool through the hole in the middle.

5. Using strong scissors, push one blade of the scissors into the wool and between the two card discs and cut the wool round the rim. You will need to help the children with this as poking the scissors in can be tricky.

6. Pass several short strands of the wool between the discs, tie them tightly round the bundle and cut off below the ends of the pompom.

7. Remove the cardboard discs and trim the top, bottom and sides of the pompom to make it flatter and more cake shaped.

x2

8 x 2m

▶

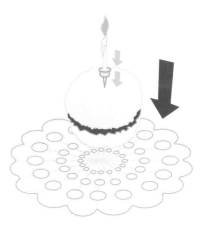

11 Using strong scissors, cut the top into a neat curve and then cut a number of small semi circles out of the triangle so that the centre of each is at the folded edge.

8 To make the candle, tightly roll up a small piece of coloured paper and glue. Then add the flame using pieces of yellow wool or felt. You can even add wax dribbles down the side of the candle using glue-gun glue.

9 To make the doily fold a square piece of paper over once into half and then into quarters...

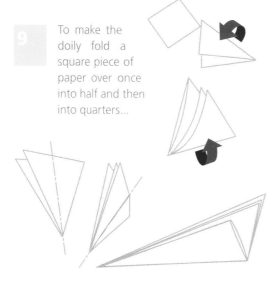

12 Unfold your doily and smooth out (or iron). Glue the candle directly into the cake or use a real birthday candle holder. Glue the candle in the holder and glue the holder into the cake.

10 ...then fold in half twice more so that you have a long thin triangle.

Get ready to make a wish...

fold-up paper shirts

So you want to be a tailor and make some of the most beautifully pressed shirts in town? Well, this is the Japanese art of paper folding (origami), with a new twist. This paper-craft couldn't be simpler and you don't need to buy any special paper. The easy-to-follow instructions show you how to fold up a shirt from a rectangular piece of office printer paper, ready for you to design and decorate however you choose. You'll also find lots of eye-catching designs for you to print and use on our website. These shirts make brilliantly original greetings cards and they are guaranteed to make a great impression and show someone that you really care. Learn the folds, and then next time you're bored at work or school, make a paper shirt from that fax from accounts, or the note from your teacher...

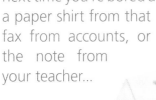

Let your imagination run wild with these fold-up paper shirts

7 years +

5 minutes

Sheet of A4 paper

download available

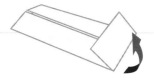

1 Place paper on a flat surface.

5 Fold the whole bottom edge over level with the folds you have just made.

2 Carefully fold in half lengthways and then unfold.

6 Unfold bottom edge you have just folded over.

7 Unfold the corners and turn them in on themselves so that they are tucked under and your piece looks like this.

3 Fold the outside edges into the centre line, taking care to make accurate folds.

8 Pull the inside of the folded in corners.

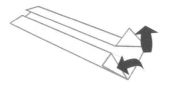

9 Press down so that corner folds along the outside edge of the piece.

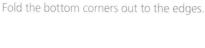

4 Fold the bottom corners out to the edges.

fold-up paper shirts

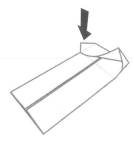

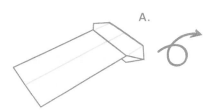

10   Press down and crease edge to make a neat triangle pointing at right angles to the edge.

11   Your piece should look like picture **A**. **Now turn it over.**

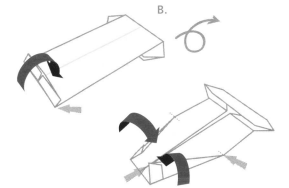

12   Fold the other edge over. Your piece should look like picture **B**. **Now turn back over.**

13   Fold top edges over so that the collar corners meet in the middle.

14   Fold the bottom of the piece up to the top so that it tucks under the collar folds and press down the bottom crease to make it permanent.

15   Your finished shirt should look like picture **C**. Get designing! You can also visit our website to print out lots of exciting shirt designs.

Why not try out one of your designs on the real thing? Paint a T-shirt on p77.

handmade
envelopes

Make yours a letter to remember

6 years +

5 minutes

Rectangular piece of paper

download available

Getting a letter in the post from a friend or someone you care about is one of life's great pleasures. Now you can make someone's day by creating your own lovely envelopes and sending one yourself.

These envelopes are really quick to make and by decorating a plain white or coloured piece of paper you can turn your letter into a real piece of art. On our website you'll find a range of patterns to print out and use, and the envelope is designed so that the pattern is on the inside, making these envelopes beautifully subtle. Whether it's Get Well Soon, Good Luck or simply a note to say Thinking of You, there's an envelope design for every occasion.

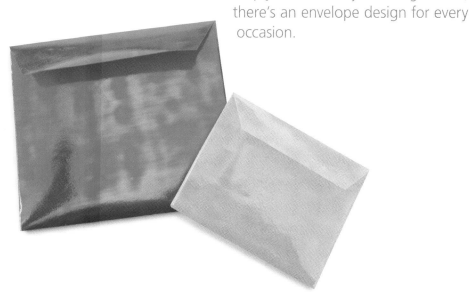

1. Take any rectangular piece of paper; gift wrapping paper is ideal. Place the side of the paper that you would like to be on the outside of the finished envelope, facing down.

2. Fold the paper neatly across the middle, but not in half. Leave enough paper poking out from underneath to form your final envelope sealing flap. For an A4 piece of printer paper this is about 20mm, for smaller sheets of paper it should be in proportion to this, as illustrated.

3. Using a ball point pen mark a straight line parallel to the two side edges, about the same distance in from each edge as the sealing flap is poking out. Press quite hard with the pen so that you crease through to the bottom bit of paper when you draw the line.

4. Cut the bottom corners off the folded paper to the line at about 60°. Cut the top corners from the top and the sides to meet at the drawn line, as illustrated, again at about 60°.

5. Unfold the paper so that the outside is facing upwards.

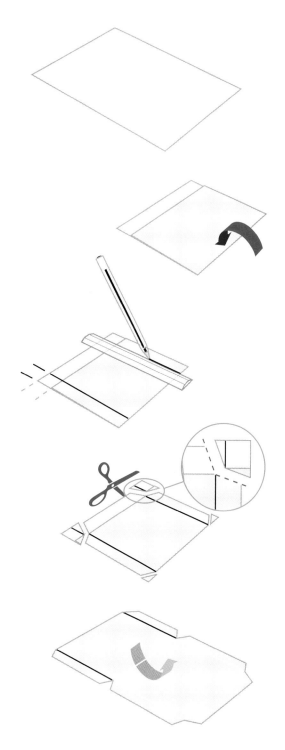

6 Carefully cutting with scissors or a craft knife and rule, cut off the flaps on only half the paper to the lines you drew. Make sure you just cut the pen lines off with the flaps.

7 Turn the paper over and fold the remaining flaps over at the creases caused by pressing through with the ballpoint pen when you drew the lines earlier.

8 Apply glue or, better still, a thin strip of double-sided tape, on each flap and peel off the backing.

9 Fold the paper over taking care to make sure that it is square and that the edges line up nicely.

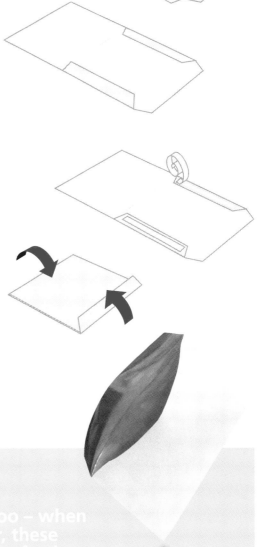

Make your letter a special one too – when made from an A4 piece of paper, these envelopes will fit a paper shirt perfectly.

BIG KITCHEN SCIENCE

The Möbius Strip is a one-sided, one-edged loop named after an astronomer and mathematician called August Möbius. Making a Möbius strip is easy, and children aged six and up will be fascinated by this look into the world of topology, the science of the surface of a 3D shape. My dad first showed me how to make a Möbius strip and I have never forgotten it, or the profound impression the idea of a piece of paper only having one side, made on me. Nor am I alone – scientists, mathematicians, engineers and artists have all been fascinated by this weird form. There are some very interesting things to consider with a Möbius strip, and despite its simplicity as a project it will get your kids thinking about how we describe forms and categorise shapes and surfaces.

It won't take you long to get started on this project. Soon you'll be able to cut two circular loops of paper along their length so that they turn into a square-edged frame before your very eyes – the nearest you're ever likely to get to being able to do magic.

Mind-bending adventures in topology

Kids love to categorise things, it helps them make sense of the world they are learning about as they grow up. It is mesmerising to them that different 3D shapes can be put into similar groups based on how many surfaces or edges they have. Kids can pick this sort of stuff up quicker than the average grown-up, because they haven't yet become entrenched in their thinking, and they'll quickly grasp concepts like this one.

6 years +

10 minutes

Sheet of paper
Scissors
Sticky tape or glue

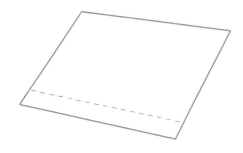

Cut a strip from the edge of a piece of plain paper.

Make a cylindrical loop shape, then twist one end 180° (ie. one half turn) so that the ends line up.

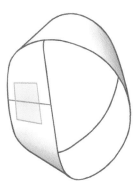

Tape the ends together, that's it.

4 Once you have made your Möbius strip you can do some cool things with it.

Try colouring it in, can you colour both sides different colours?

Try cutting it in half lengthways, you'll find something very strange happens.

5 Stick a Möbius strip at right angles to a untwisted loop, then cut these in half lengthways. You'll get a square frame – weird or what?

6 Stick a Möbius strip at right angles to another Möbius strip with a twist in the opposite direction.

You'll get two linked hearts – sweet science!

When did MC Escher draw his famous Möbius Strip picture?

The artist MC Escher loved the idea of the Möbius Strip and used it as the basis for his drawing *Möbius Strip II (Red Ants)*, completed in 1963. In the picture the red ants keep walking round the strip but can never find the other side of it.

How is the Möbius Strip used practically in industry?

The lifespan of conveyor belts is doubled through use of this concept, as the belt gets worn over its whole area and not just one side.

What is topology?

Topology is the branch of geometry that deals with the study of the surface of a 3D shape. In topology, shapes are grouped into similar forms which all have the same number of surfaces, and not necessarily by their actual shape. In topology a coffee mug can be described as a form of torus, or doughnut, because although it looks completely different, the coffee mug and doughnut actually share the same type of surfaces, only in the mug one side of the doughnut has been dented in.

Where can I see a Möbius Strip?

Did you know that the world-wide symbol for recycling is in fact a Möbius Strip?

Make the most of a holiday

When the holidays come, millions of separated dads and their kids spend more time together. It's a time of year that all single dads look forward to, a time to trade the morsel of 'staying access' for a proper slice of family life. However, spending a whole week together with your children is not simply an extended version of a weekend overnight stay. Here are ten tips that will help you get the most out of this special, extra time you spend with your children.

Negotiate sensibly and early

Make a note of what you agree. It's easy to forget the detail of arrangements later, especially if you agreed them months before. Be fair and flexible; remember you and your ex-partner both have holiday needs. If your ex-partner has work commitments try to take some days leave to share out the holiday childcare.

Don't over-promise

Don't oversell the holiday to your children or get competitive about who is going to give them the best time. You may be staying at home with your children while your ex-partner is taking them abroad, or the other way round, but remember that you both just want your children to have a lovely time whoever they're with, and wherever they are.

Plan the time

If you're going away, choose and plan the holiday with your children. If you're staying at home, make a rough daily plan before the holiday starts; outings, a picnic, a family barbeque, a film or a making and doing day, for example. Be flexible, the plan is only your guide.

Plan the food

A week of providing three meals a day will be a shock if you are not used to that routine. Don't spend the week eating takeaways or sitting in restaurants; plan to cook for them, they'll love it. Strike the balance between wholesome food and treats, but cook food that you know they like.

Be prepared for minor illnesses

You only have a few days so it would be a pity to waste them on headaches, tummy upsets and sunburn. A change in a child's routine can cause problems which are often expressed as minor ailments like headaches and tummy upsets. Stock a basic medicine box like the one described on p89, and make sure your kids are wearing sun cream.

Make a packing list

If you are going away for a week, or even just a couple of days, start a packing list and get out the suitcase a

steam train PAGE 112

sugar mice PAGE 196

few days before the holiday. Put things on the list or in the suitcase as you think of them. For young children and even those up to the age of about 10 or 11 years old, remember to pack a favourite teddy or cuddly toy.

7 Promote contact

Encourage your child to phone, email or send a postcard to their mother. Help them to do this, especially if they are very young, but give them their privacy if they want to speak on the phone or write something in private. Avoid the temptation to try and overhear what they are saying on the phone, and don't question them about what was said after they have hung up unless they look distressed. Understand that they will be missing their mother and that this doesn't reflect on the holiday or how much they love you.

8 Don't quiz them about their other home

On an extended stay, you are likely to relax into longer and more interesting conversations. This is a great time to get to know your children, but don't use this opportunity to quiz them about their mother. Listen to them and take in what they have to say. If you want to know more about their life (and you should) then ask them about their school and their friends and get to know the sort of things they do while you're not around.

9 Relax

Don't try to do too much in this holiday. Pace yourself, there will be other holidays, other weeks. Putting too much pressure on this time will only spoil it. If you've planned and you're prepared, then just relax and enjoy yourself. Be yourself with your kids. Remember, this is one more step in the growth of a relationship that has a lifetime to develop.

10 Be yourself

Resist the temptation to spoil your kids with expensive treats and gifts. These are not a substitute for your time and love, and you're their dad, not a toy shop. Your kids love you because you're their father and you're there, just for them.

love heart gift box PAGE 188

There are three stages of a man's life:
He believes in Santa Claus;
He doesn't believe in Santa Claus;
He is Santa Claus.

UNKNOWN

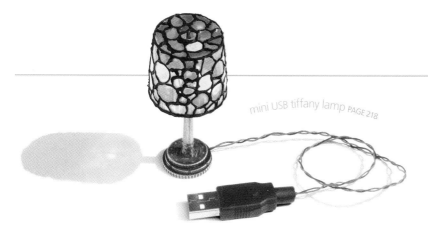

mini USB tiffany lamp PAGE 218

victorian domed display case PAGE 236

samurai sword PAGE 230

mini USB
tiffany lamp

Make this fabulous miniature USB Tiffany lamp from a bottle cap

12 years +

2 hours

3 x Small copper coins
Paintbrush end
Marker
Emery paper
Superglue
Low cost USB LED lamp
Glue-gun glue
Paper clip
Bottle cap
Glass paint
Stained glass black craft outline
Soldering iron

Tiffany lamps are those beautiful coloured-glass lamps originally made by Louis Comfort Tiffany at the beginning of the 20th century. Original Tiffany lamps command huge prices at auction, but now you can make one for yourself from a bottle cap, three coins and the metal end of an old paintbrush.

The shade is made from a small clear or transluscent bottle cap. You can paint any Art Nouveau pattern on the outside and all you need are some coloured permanent markers in red, yellow and green for the design and a black marker or embossing pen for outlining the pattern. The lamp glows wonderfully with the super-bright LED, easily hacked from a very cheap mini USB PC light. The LED light is just perfect as a starting point for making your lamp and contains everything you'll need to make the light work properly: the LED with the correct resistor, a short length of wire and the USB plug.

mini USB tiffany lamp

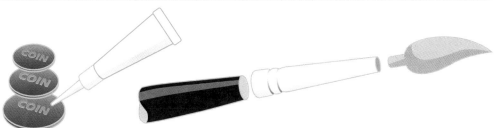

1 Take three small copper (or silver) coins of diminishing size and superglue them together, so that they are centred with respect to each other, in a nice neat pile.

4 The stem of the lamp is made from a small paintbrush ferrule. Carefully remove the bristles and then either pull out or drill out the handle using a small gauge drill bit. If the bristles are glued in firmly, then the only way to remove them will be to cut them off at the tip of the ferrule and drill them out as well. When drilling, hold the ferrule gently in a vice to avoid injury.

2 Using black spray paint or a permanent black marker, colour the coins all over.

5 Once you have removed the handle and the bristles, you will have a nice, miniature, tapering metal tube. Using a pair of pliers or other metal object, bend up a small part of the end of the ferrule (this is to let the wire out once the ferrule has been stuck to the coins).

3 Using the finest sandpaper you have, or wet and dry emery paper, rub down the coins to remove the black from all the edges and the top of the uppermost coin.

6 To make the lampshade support you will need one medium sized paperclip. Carefully straighten out two of the loops as shown.

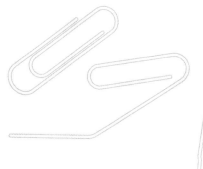

▶

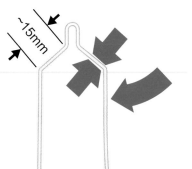

7 Using a pair of pliers, squeeze the remaining loop until it is only about 2 or 3mm wide (see the template below for a bending guide). To use the guide, hold the wire up against the page and mark off the bends on to the wire with a permanent marker before bending.

9 Grip the wire so the the edge of the pliers is about 15mm down the sloping edge and bend the legs down to vertical on both sides.

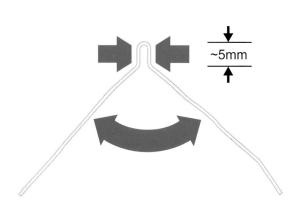

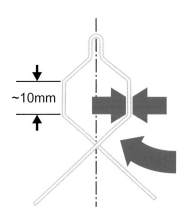

8 Holding the squeezed loop tightly with the pliers, fold up the two legs to about 45° so that they are even and the narrow loop is about 5mm deep.

10 Now grip the wire so that the bottom edge of the pliers is about 10mm down the vertical parts and bend them back at 45° so that they cross at the centre point.

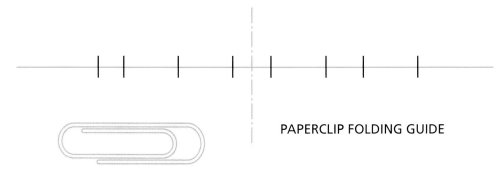

PAPERCLIP FOLDING GUIDE

~13mm

11 Finally, grip the wire so that the bottom edge of the pliers is about 13mm down the sloping part and bend the legs back to the vertical so that they are level in the centre.

12 Preparing the LED lamp is easy. Cut the USB plug off a standard (low cost) USB laptop light. You will need strong pliers to cut through the spring and wire coating.

13 Remove the lens and slip out the LED.

14 Thread the LED wires through the ferrule and lay them so that they exit at the bottom of the tube, through the small gap you turned up earlier.

15 Carefully thread the paper-clip lampshade holder into the end of the ferrule and pull the LED down so that it sits in the middle of the wire shape, but does not short out on the metal parts.

quick setting epoxy resin or glue-gun glue

16 Use quick setting resin or glue-gun glue to seal up the base of the ferrule. If using glue-gun glue, then hold the ferrule with a tissue, because it is metal and will get hot when you squeeze the glue down inside it.

17 Use resin or superglue (cyanoacrylate) to glue the ferrule to the coin base. **DO NOT LET CHILDREN USE CYANOACRYLATE GLUE (SUPERGLUE).** Slip the lens back on to the LED to act as a diffuser.

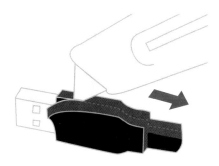

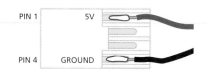

21 When looking at the plug from the side that you are going to solder, the pins are arranged like this. Take care to get it right, you shouldn't be able to harm your computer, but if you get it round the wrong way the LED will not light up.

glue-gun glue

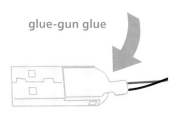

18 To take the moulded USB plug apart, carefully slit the rubbery plastic on one side and peel the plug moulding off the inner metal part. Inside the plug will have a metal case, unfold the metal grips where the wire comes out of the plug and carefully remove the top part of the metal case.

22 When you have soldered the wires back on to the plug, get ready to replace the metal case top part. Put a small amount of glue-gun glue inside the plug to pot the wires nicely and while the glue is still soft, clip the top case back on and bend the gripper round the neck of the metal case.

RUBBERY OUTER

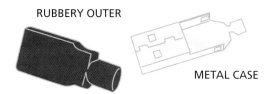

METAL CASE

cyanoacrylate

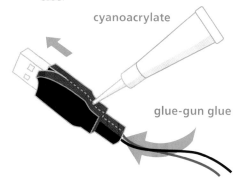

glue-gun glue

19 Inside the metal case there will be more rubber. You must remove all the rubber carefully without damaging the plug. When removing the rubber you will break the delicate wires that go to the 5v and ground pins. No worries, you are going to solder new ones on anyway.

PLASTIC PIN CHASSIS

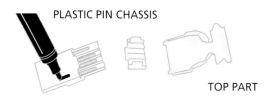

TOP PART

20 Just to be sure, mark the plug pin that had the black wire coming from it using a permanent black marker.

23 Put some glue-gun glue round the wire end of the USB plug assembly and slip the rubber USB plug cover back round the metal case. Glue up using superglue. **NEVER LET CHILDREN USE CYANO-ACRYLATE (SUPERGLUE).**

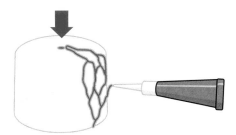

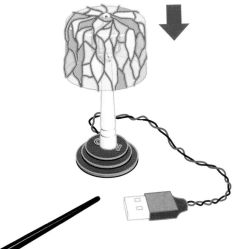

24 A small clear or transluscent bottle cap or personal healthcare product closure may be used for the lampshade. Drill a small (3mm diameter) hole in the centre of the top of the cap. Draw the stained glass pattern on to the cap with a special tube of craft stained glass liner (liquid lead).

26 Rest the lampshade on the lampshade holder. Glue it on if you like, or leave it unglued so that you can make a range of different lampshades.

25 Fill in the leaded light glass panels with transparent or glass paint. Use as many colours as you can to make a really bright and colourful lampshade.

Make the miniature lampshade from almost anything you like – paper, tracing paper, OHP film, or tissue. You could even make a Chinese lantern!

mini USB spotlight

12 years +

2 hours

Soldering iron
Glue gun
Superglue
Double-sided sticky tape
Silver paint

This project starts with a USB laptop light, which can be bought very cheaply online. A simple spotlight like this is the perfect way to start beginners soldering and making electrical circuits, but do take care as soldering irons get very hot and will give you a nasty burn if mishandled. Supervise children at all times, turn off the soldering iron immediately after use and do not leave any trailing flex. Part of this project also requires superglue and should therefore be done carefully by an adult.

I used a translucent cap from a cheap supermarket shampoo bottle, but any translucent round (barrel-shaped) cap will do. It is best to use translucent plastic because the real spotlight has heat dissipation vents at the side and these let some light out, which gives the spotlight those characteristic glowing rings.

When your light is finished, shine it up on to the wall, and you'll see you get an absolutely fantastic effect.

mini USB spotlight

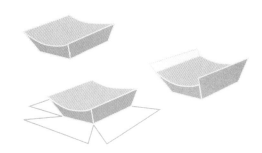

1 For this project you will need a small translucent barrel, I used a cheap shampoo bottle closure.

2 Make the closure neat and round, cut off the flip top lid it you need to. Coat some thick tin foil in double-sided sticky tape on one side, and cut into five thin strips and stick them evenly spaced round the cap.

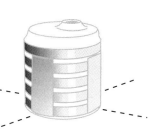

3 Cut some shorter, slightly wider strips and stick these along the length of the barrel at 90° spacing.

4 Carve the power converter from a piece of wine bottle cork or something similar and cover with foil, leave the side edges long so that they hide any poor joins.

5 Attach to the side of the barrel in line with what will become the bottom of the lamp.

6 Colour in the top of the bottle lid. This will be the back end of the spotlight. Spray, paint or use a silver pen to colour it in. **DO NOT** colour the sides between the strips.

▶

7 Cut the USB plug off the standard USB laptop light. You will need to use strong pliers to cut through the spring and wire coating.

8 Remove the light lens and slip out the LED.

glue-gun glue

glue-gun glue

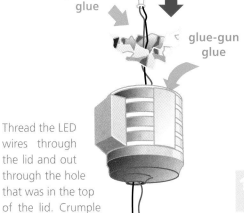

9 Thread the LED wires through the lid and out through the hole that was in the top of the lid. Crumple some foil and glue in the base of the spotlight to act as a reflector, making sure that the wires aren't shorted on to it.

10 To take a moulded-on plug apart, carefully slit the rubbery plastic on one side and peel the plug moulding off the inner metal part. Inside the plug will have a metal case, unfold the metal grips where the wire comes out of the plug and carefully remove the top part of the metal case.

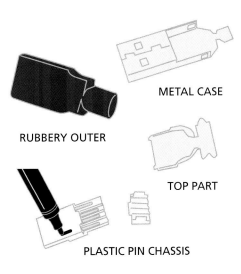

METAL CASE

RUBBERY OUTER

TOP PART

PLASTIC PIN CHASSIS

11 Inside the metal case there will be more rubber. You must remove all the rubber carefully without damaging the plug. When removing the rubber you will break the delicate wires that go to the 5v and ground pins. No worries, you are going to solder new ones on anyway.

SERIES A USB PLUG

| PIN 1 | 5V |
| PIN 4 | GROUND |

mini USB spotlight

12 When looking at the plug from the side that you are going to solder, the pins are arranged like this. Take care to get it right, you shouldn't be able to harm your computer, but if you get it round the wrong way the LED will not light up.

glue-gun glue

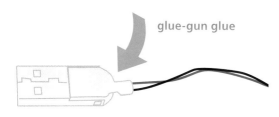

13 When you have soldered the wires back on to the plug, get ready to replace the metal case top part. Put a small amount of glue-gun glue inside the plug to pot the wires nicely and while the glue is still soft, clip the top case back on and bend the gripper round the neck of the metal case.

cyanoacrylate

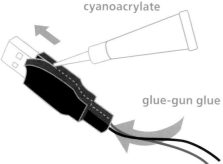

glue-gun glue

14 Put some glue-gun glue round the wire end of the USB plug assembly and slip the rubber USB plug cover back round the metal case. Glue up using superglue (cyanoacrylate). **NEVER LET CHILDREN USE CYANOACRYLATE (SUPERGLUE).**

15 Place some transparent film over the top of the spotlight and mark a circle very slightly smaller than the inside diameter of the lamp. Mark three small tabs then cut out the lens with scissors.

16 Mark out and then cut out the bat logo so that it is big enough to fit across the spotlight lens and then cut a strip of foil to line the inside of the spotlight.

double-sided sticky tape

17 Stick the bat logo to the front of the lens with double-sided sticky tape and fold the tabs down and put a small piece of double sided sticky tape on each one. Do not peel off the backing.

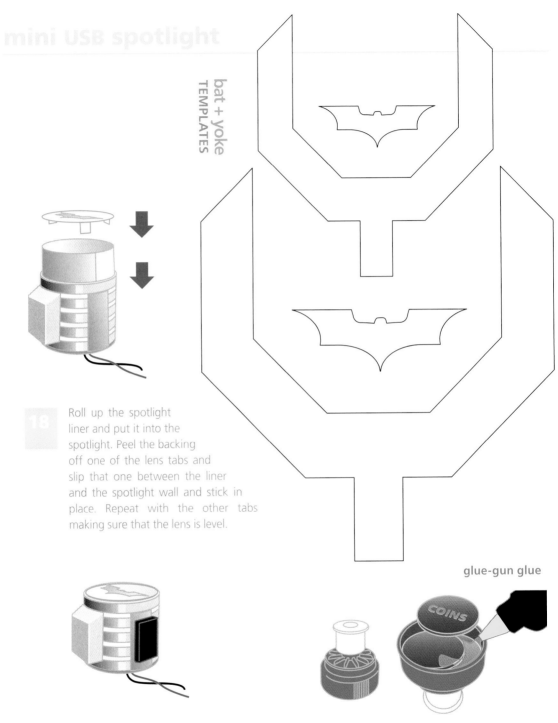

bat + yoke
TEMPLATES

glue-gun glue

COINS

18 Roll up the spotlight liner and put it into the spotlight. Peel the backing off one of the lens tabs and slip that one between the liner and the spotlight wall and stick in place. Repeat with the other tabs making sure that the lens is level.

19 Cut some small stiff card rectangles and colour in black with a permanent marker and glue-gun glue one to either side of the spotlight.

20 Fill the inside of a single serving drinks sport bottle top with old coins to give it some weight. Glue in with glue-gun glue.

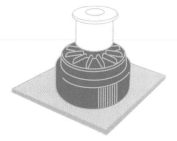

21 Fill with coins and glue-gun glue and before it sets, place right way up on some stiff card and leave to set.

22 Using the templates and measuring against your spotlight diameter mark out the shape of the yoke on a piece of thick, stiff card, like foamcore.

23 Carefully cut out the yoke. To make this thick and strong you may need to stick two or more pieces of card together.

24 Glue the yoke into the single serving bottle cap and spray or paint black.

25 Stick the spotlight in the yoke at the appropriate angle. The yoke will rotate using the drinking cap mechanism, but if you want it to pitch as well then secure to the yoke with pins or small nails.

glue-gun glue

The perfect way to start beginners soldering and making electrical circuits.

samurai sword

Making this wooden-bladed Samurai sword or *katana* will elevate you to the status of a legendary swordsmith

10 years +

90 minutes

1m x 32mm Plastic waste pipe
2 x 40mm Cupboard door knobs
4m x 12mm Black webbing
Sink strainer
1m Wood strip
Gold and colour spray paint

A Samurai sword is a true work of art. The technique of making the blade by heating the metal up and cooling it down repeatedly was used to purify the metal, and the results, even in the 13th and 14th century with ancient forging equipment, were amazing. Modern swords are judged not to be as good as those made hundreds of years ago by the great Japanese swordsmiths. Samurai swords have become renowned for their sharpness and cutting ability, and even though the blade on our sword isn't metal, the smoothly finished hardwood does have a satisfyingly Japanese feel to it. And, of course, you wouldn't really want your kids running round with a high carbon steel sword so sharp it could dice concrete.

samurai sword

1 Because the paint will take some time to dry, the first thing you must do is prepare the pipe and paint it. The pipe is going to be the handle (TSUKA) and the scabbard (SAYA), so take about 1 metre of plastic waste pipe and cut it in two roughly 30cm from one end. Make sure that the cut is at right angles to the length of the pipe and not on a slant.

2 Sandpaper the surface of the plastic pipe with a fine grade of sandpaper to rough up the surface and provide a key for the paint. Paint or spray the long part black, brown or bright red. Spray down inside one end a little bit, because this will be the mouth of the scabbard. Spray the short part gold or silver. Use a bottle to hold the pipe while it dries.

3 Cut the sword blade (KEN) and tang (the bit that fits inside the handle) (NAGAGO) from a single strip of hardwood, such as oak or beech 29mm x 10mm. Cut the wood so that it is a bit shorter than the plastic pipe bits together (about 92cm). There is no need to make a dangerous point, just cut the corner off the end for an authentic look.

4 Sandpaper the wood with medium and then fine sandpaper to give a slightly rounded edge to the blade (KEN). Take care not to get splinters in your fingers as you rub the sandpaper up and down the blade. Only sandpaper the visible part of the blade.

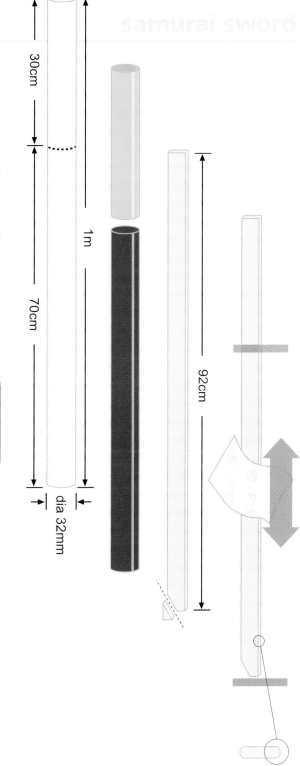

30cm

1m

70cm

dia 32mm

92cm

GLUE

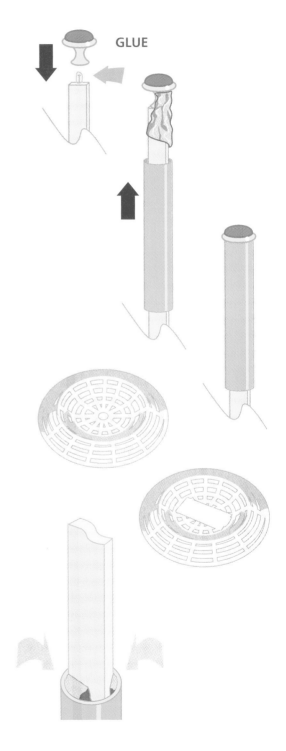

5 Hammer a small nail into the centre of the end of the wooden strip at the handle end and glue the door knob on to the end of the wood. This is only a temporary fixing to hold the door knob steady while you do the next stage.

6 Mix up some car body or decorators resin filler (two part epoxy filler) and spread it neatly round the join between the door knob and the wood end. Quickly, and before the resin has set, slide the handle pipe part over the wood and up to the door knob.

7 When the resin is in its rubbery pre-setting stage, trim off any bits that have squeezed out of the join to make the join between the door knob and the pipe handle part neat and free of resin. Let the resin set hard (15mins) before moving on to the next stage.

8 A sink plug strainer makes an ideal guard (TSUBA) and because you are using waste pipe to make the handle and scabbard, you'll find that a sink strainer should be a good fit with your handle.

9 Cut out a rectangular hole in the flat part of the strainer, the size of your blade. Most strainers these days are metal plated plastic. If you have one of these, then all you will need is a pair of scissors to cut the hole. If you have a metal one, you will need tin snips and or a metal file.

10 To fix the handle and make it feel really solid, mix up some more two part resin and neatly fill out the other end of the handle pipe, round the wooden blade.

11 Before it sets push the guard on to the blade and slide it down to rest on the top on the handle end.

12 Either using more of the two part resin you have just mixed up or using some new resin, put a small amount round the end of the handle area over the inner part of the strainer guard so that the resin goes through the strainer holes and bonds to the resin that is packing out the end of the handle.

13 Now it's time to fit the end cap to the scabbard. Using another door knob coat the end of the door knob and the inside of the scabbard pipe in two part resin.

14 Gently push the door knob into the end of the scabbard pipe. Remove any excess resin.

15 Quickly turn the pipe over so that the uncured resin doesn't run down inside the scabbard. Rest the door knob on the floor and keep the scabbard vertical until the resin has set (usually 10 to 15 minutes, depending on how much hardener you used when mixing it up).

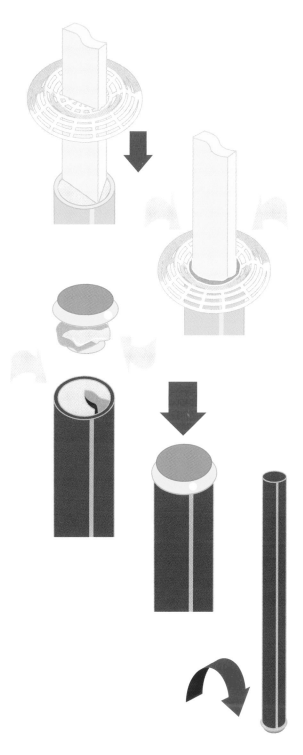

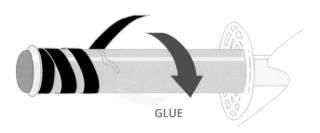

GLUE

16 To achieve that distinctive look that is normally made from carefully overlapping the braid (ITO), you are going to wrap the handle in a narrow webbing. Any colour will do, but black looks really good. Start winding the webbing round the handle in a spiral, keeping the gaps between the webbing even and about half the width of the webbing apart. Lay a strip of glue under the webbing as you go and keep the webbing tight. This is a two person job. Hot melt (glue gun) glue is the best for this. Seal any cut ends of the webbing with a lighted match to stop them fraying.

GLUE

18 The cord (SAGEO) was used to tie back clothing when the sword bearer was about to fight. Ninjas had longer cords and would use the cord to hold the sword in their teeth so as to keep both hands free for climbing. To make the cord, glue down some webbing and double it over itself and glue down again so that it looks like a bow.

GLUE

17 When you reach the end, go once round the handle completely to cover up the end of the handle and then start spiralling back up the handle. Take care to keep the space between the windings even and the same as the windings going the other way, so that the diamond shapes created by the counterwise wrapping are in a straight line.

samurai sword

GLUE

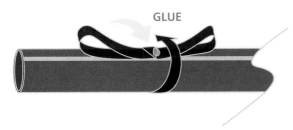

19 Fold over the webbing strip at 45° and wrap the webbing round the scabbard twice in the same place so that a bit of thickness builds up. Glue the webbing every half turn.

GLUE

20 After the second wrap, on top of the bow move the web across so that you can make another wrap next to the first (about one strap's width apart). Wrap the webbing strap around twice again in the new spot to create a second thick band. Cut the webbing off and seal the end with a lighted match (an adult must do this part) then glue down. Now sheath your sword and you are ready to play – carefully now.

Become a heroic samurai swordsmith in just 90 minutes!

victorian domed display case

An authentic-looking Victorian clear display dome made from an old bottle

10 years +

1 hour

Glue gun
Black paint
Christmas bauble
Large plastic fizzy
drink bottle
Felt

When you make something beautiful or bring back a memento from a long adventure, nothing is better than displaying your prized possession as the centrepiece of a mantle-shelf arrangement. In Victorian times, elegant drawing rooms up and down the land would have been stuffed to the gills with all kinds of nick-nacks, neatly laid out to cover almost every available surface.

This project is the perfect way to display all your most beautiful holiday trinkets and the things that you make. It will keep the dust off them and show them off in a really special way. The best bit is that it's a quick little project, and all you need is some cardboard, a Christmas bauble or something similar and an empty two-litre plastic drinks bottle.

Your kids will love this project and as the dome isn't glued down, you can lift it off just like in a real display case, and change the object whenever you feel like it.

victorian domed display case

1 Take one 2 litre drink bottle and cut it halfway down near the bottom and at the top. Avoid scratching or marking the upper part of the bottle, which is going to be the 'glass' dome. Remove any label adhesive residue with nail varnish remover or cellulose thinners and then polish the dome with furniture polish.

2 Use a hack saw to cut off the top and hold the top rather than the bottle.

3 Using the base part draw a circle on a suitable piece of thick card taking care not to squeeze the plastic base into an oval. Cut the card out so that it is the same diameter as the bottle.

4 Use a large yoghurt pot or similar tapering food pot for the product stand. Cut off to a suitable height so that the base fits easily inside the dome and cut a large hole in the upturned bottom.

5 Glue the plastic pot base centrally to the cardboard and fill with some screws glue-gun glued in position to give it weight.

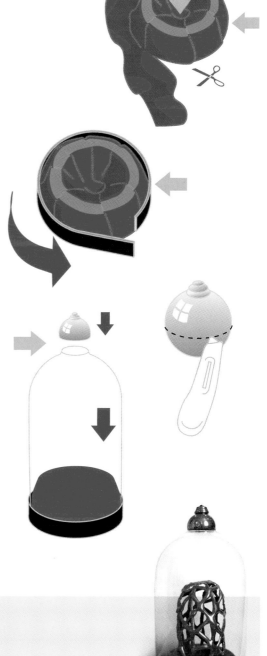

6 Cover with suitable fabric (velvet) by glueing fabric down in the middle and then pulling taut all round and glueing to the edge of the cardboard. When glue is dry trim off flush with the base of the cardboard.

7 Cut a strip of card about 15mm wide. Paint or spray it black and then glue it round the covered card base so the bottom edge is flush with the base of the card.

8 To cover up the cut top of the drink bottle, use a plastic Christmas bauble decoration with a metalised finish, cut in half.

9 Stick the decoration to the top of the soda bottle dome to cover up the cut top. Remove the Christmas decoration loop, or if there is a hole in the top of the decoration cover with a blob of glue-gun glue or a stick on craft gem.

Go back in time with this stylish glass dome – a classic way to present the things you've made.

victoriana tennis rackets

Practice low passing shots over the sofa and volley to win in your own Centre Court playing with this lovely project.

The scroll work is what makes a simple piece of card not only look beautiful, but strong enough to bat a lightweight ball back and forth. You can print a beautiful template from our website, but once you see how to make the rackets, why not design your own scroll work. As long as you make sure that there are a few strips that go from the handle up and across the racket face, you can make the design anything you want: a butterfly, a shamrock, a love heart, or your national flag! The list is endless.

The project also shows you how to make a pompom ball from a piece of card and a couple of plastic carrier bags. The resulting ball is resilient enough to bat about as hard as you like, and yet soft enough to play with indoors.

Become a world champion on grass or carpet with these gorgeous gilded tennis rackets

8 years +

2 hours

Cardboard
Felt
Carrier bag
Clear plastic sheet

download available

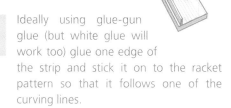

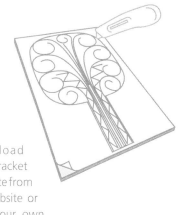

1 Download the racket template from our website or draw your own design. Stick it onto some thick corrugated card using white glue and carefully cut it out.

4 Ideally using glue-gun glue (but white glue will work too) glue one edge of the strip and stick it on to the racket pattern so that it follows one of the curving lines.

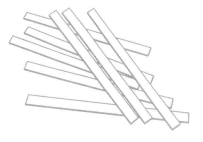

2 Accurately cut some strips of thinner corrugated or lightweight card. If you use corrugated make sure to cut the strips across the flutes (not along them).

5 Repeat for all the strips. For more complex shapes fold up the shape and pinch it together so you can apply the glue more easily to its edge.

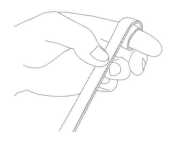

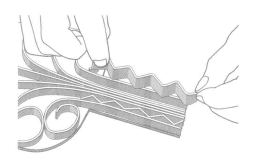

3 Curl up the end of a strip by wrapping it tightly round your finger.

6 Carefully glue all the strips on to the rackets to follow all the lines.

victoriana tennis rackets

7 Either follow the pattern or add bits in to the pattern to make it more intricate if you want.

8 When you have stuck strips over all the lines, spray or paint the racket all over. You can use any colour, but silver or gold look really nice, and give the effect of gilded wrought metalwork.

9 Carefully apply glue to the top edge of the strips and cover the racket with a thin sheet of clear plastic from some old packaging, or an overhead projector slide.

10 Carefully draw the shape of the racket on to the plastic layer using a permanent marker, then cut out round the edge using strong scissors.

11 Neatly draw over the glued cardboard edge using a gold or silver marker. This hides the glued edge and makes the scroll-work look much neater.

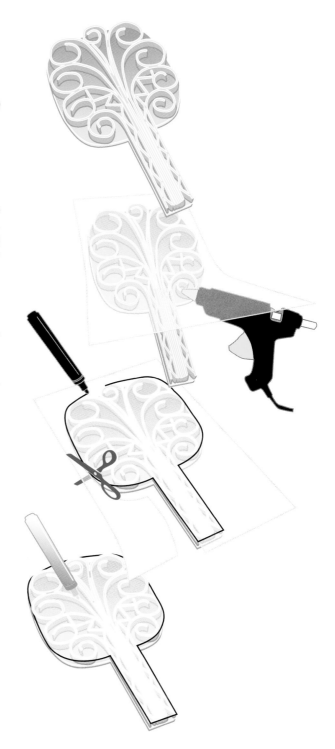

12 Cut a strip of felt, material or leather the same thickness as the racket and glue round the edge. Glue it to the outer bulges of the scrollwork swirls.

13 Repeat for the other racket. Use a different design for the scrollwork if you want or a contrasting colour for the edge strip material.

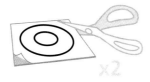

14 Trace the pompom disc templates from p40 and stick them to a stiff piece of thin cardboard. Cut round the circle and cut out the hole in the middle.

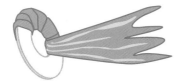

15 Cut a thin plastic carrier bag in half lengthways and hold the two discs together, then wrap the plastic round the discs by poking it through the hole repeatedly. Make sure you wrap it nice and tightly.

16 Keep wrapping it round until you can't poke it through the hole in the middle any more. Use more than one carrier bag if you need to.

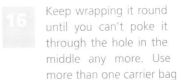

17 Start with a knife if you have to, but then using strong sharp scissors cut round the edge of the wrapped disc. Poke the scissors in between the two card discs.

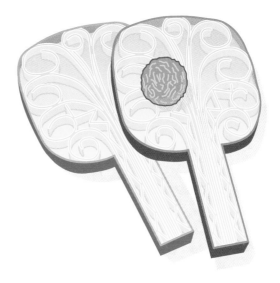

18 Use a length of plastic bag doubled over, or some string, and passing it between the discs tie off as tightly as possible.

20 You're all ready to play. Because the ball is nice and soft, this game is safe to play indoors or outdoors.

19 Trim off the ties and then trim the pompom to make sure it is as round as possible. Don't pull out any straggling bits of plastic, just trim them off.

While away any rain-stopped-play afternoons during Wimbledon!

gel cell battery

Make a real battery that will power a clock from stuff that you find round the kitchen

12 years +

2–3 hours

Empty 35mm film containers
Salt
Vinegar
Gelatin (or fruit jelly)
Absorbent paper
Copper wire
Aluminium cooking foil
Kitchen scissors
Craft knife
Pliers

download available

This experiment involves mixing salt, vinegar and jelly. It's satisfyingly challenging, but certainly not beyond any older child / dad team. The effort is well worth it, and unlike the typical wet cell homemade battery, this design is really compact and looks and works just like the real thing. The experiment can be used as a basis for some interesting discussions about the mechanism of electricity generation.

We made four cells so that we could get a mechanical clock working, however, if you only want to make one or two cells you might try using them to power a simple low-power LCD clock. Our website has printable labels so that you can make your batteries look just like the real thing!

gel cell battery

1. Strip about 2m of multi strand copper wire.

2. Cut out 12 strips of aluminium baking foil approx 25mm x 300mm.

3. Lay the foil strips in four piles of three pieces and twist together about 30mm of one end and fold the twisted part out at right angles.

4. Cut out four strips of blotting paper, or absorbent kitchen paper towel, approx 40mm x 500mm.

5. Make a mark on the paper at the halfway point. Then on one half, carefully lay out a 500mm length of the bared copper strands, doubling it back and tacking it lightly at each end with a spot of glue-gun glue. Twist together about 30mm at the end of the wire and bend out at right angles to the paper. The paper part is called the separator and stops the two electrodes touching and making a short circuit.

6. Fold the paper separator over to cover the copper wire.

7. Lay one of the aluminium piles on top of the paper.

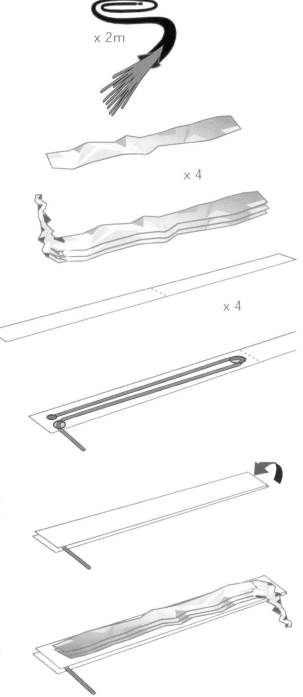

x 2m

x 4

x 4

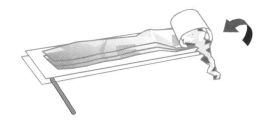

x 4

8 Roll up the sandwich taking care to make sure that no strands of copper poke out. If they do, tuck them back in, they must not touch the aluminium anywhere.

Use an old 35mm film tub for the battery casing, or cut and roll up a toilet paper tube and seal one end with a slice off a wine bottle cork (seal with glue-gun glue). **11**

9 Secure the roll with a small piece of sticky tape.

Your completed cell roll should look like this:

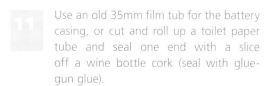

GEL ELECTROLYTE RECIPE: **10**

3 teaspoons gelatin
(Or pack, 135g, of fruit jelly)
1 tablespoon salt
2 tablespoons vinegar
150ml tap water

Make up about 150ml of jelly. Put jelly or gelatin with vinegar and heat in the microwave on high for 10 seconds and stir, then add 150ml of cold water.

Put the rolled up cell in the casing. **12**

Cut a rectangular hole in the film tub cap big enough for the copper wire and aluminium twisted end to poke through. **13**

gel cell battery

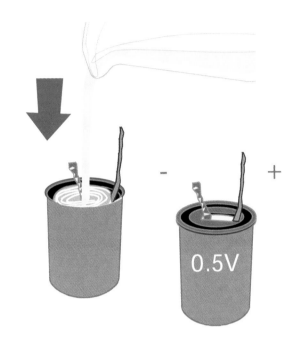

14 Carefully and slowly pour the gel electrolyte mix into the middle of the rolled up battery cell. Do not fill to the brim as the mix will bubble as a reaction starts at each electrode. As the bubbles form, the cell will float up a little, leave for about 20 minutes, then gently push the cell down and top up with a tiny bit of the electrolyte mix.

15 Carefully put the cap on the tub so that the electrodes poke out of it and are not touching. This cell will generate between about 0.5v and 0.6v. This is not a very strong battery and will not produce more than about 3mA or 4mA. Connect the batteries together in series (ie. connect the positive of one battery to the negative of another) using three strands of copper wire twisted together and tied in a granny knot round the electrodes.

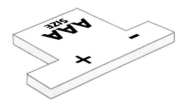

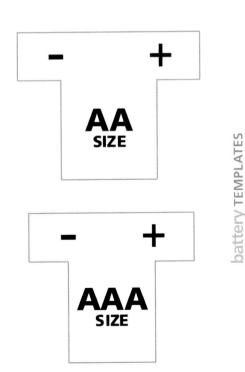

battery TEMPLATES

16 Trace and cut out the two template battery and holder shapes. The cross bar of the T is correctly sized for either an AA or an AAA battery.

17 Stick the templates to a piece of stiff, thick card (corrugated card is good or foamboard if you have it).

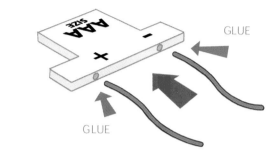

GLUE

GLUE

18 Make two small holes in the top edge and glue-gun glue a piece of copper wire into each hole.

19 Bend the wires round the edge of the card and glue-gun glue to secure on the back edge.

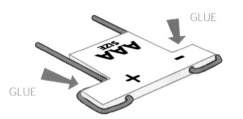

GLUE

GLUE

20 Connect to output wires of your battery array by twisting the wires together (to the correct polarity).

21 Now you can test your battery as a replacement for any 1.5v single cell.

22 Four batteries will be enough to replace an AA or AAA 1.5v battery in most low drain applications (LCD clock or MP3 player). Your battery might only run for a few minutes or a few days, but then it didn't cost $20m to develop! If you want a stronger battery look on the web and experiment with the electrode materials.

In 1831 Michael Faraday built the first electric dynamo – a simple form of generator – and showed that electricity could be generated mechanically rather than just chemically.

BIG KITCHEN SCIENCE

And they're off! A broad bean is the ideal starting point for a seed-growing experiment. Big and full of all the stuff a plant needs to get growing quickly, beans are often used in schools to teach students about germination and what happens when a dormant seed starts to grow into a new plant. This experiment is a neat twist on that time-honoured tradition, because by growing the beans down into water in clear tubes (instead of in soil) you can watch the progress of the roots as they develop. Even better, you can line up your beans and race them against each other.

Growing a plant from a seed is a great experimental project because there's something weirdly magic about it, and yet it is really proper science. On p252 you can see what the beans look like after one week. The bean at the far end had seven drops of a liquid plant food, and the bean in the middle had only one drop, but was accidentally put into the tube upside down (with respect to the growing shoot) so the leaves are trying to grow down into the water. The nearest bean had no drops of liquid feed at all and is growing in plain water.

Ready, steady, grow.

To avoid disappointment the beans are pre-soaked, and more beans than you need for the experiment are pre-germinated in a special little incubator. This is a long-term project. Once set up in their tubes, the beans will continue to grow for weeks, so your children can keep coming back to check progress. To make it even more scientific, why not selectively add a few drops of plant nutrient to the tubes, or grow different kinds of beans in each tube?

6 years +

1 month

Clear poly-tubing
Cardboard
Broad beans
Craft knife
Sealable container
Dressmaker's pins
Marker

Put some nice big fat broad beans in a bowl of water and leave for 24 hrs.

While you are waiting for the shoots to appear, make the race track. Get some clear poly-tubing with a internal diameter just a little bit bigger than the width of the beans. Broad beans are big, so you'll probably need the biggest clear tubing you can get (I used 19mm diameter tubing). Cut tubing into three same size lengths, about 450mm long.

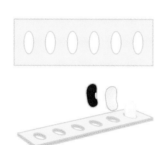

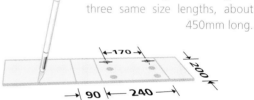

Roughly cut out a cardboard strip, cut some holes in it that just fit the beans, and gently poke the beans into it, so that they are all standing up.

Make the tubing holder from a single wide strip of card folded round, or separate pieces glue-gun glued together. For 19mm tubing, the box needs to be at least 90mm high and the holes need to be about 170mm apart, to allow the tubing to bend round easily. If you want to paint the cardboard, paint it now, before you assemble the rest of the experiment.

Put a wet kitchen towel into the bottom of a sealable plastic box, place the beans and cardboard support in the box, close the lid and put it somewhere warm and light. Inspect the beans every day until shoots appear.

Poke the tubing through the holes and arrange in neat, semicircular curves.

Crease and then fold the box section round under the tubes and glue permanently.

To stop the beans falling down the tubes, push a dressmaker's pin through each tube wall, all the way through one wall and partially into the other opposite one, about three quarters of a bean-length down the length of tubing. When your beans have started to sprout take them out of their incubator and gently place one in the end of each tube resting on the pin.

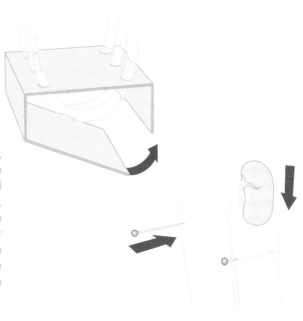

9 Carefully fill the tubes up with water to just below the dressmaker's needles. To follow the growth of the bean root, mark the tubes with ballpoint pen or permanent marker each day. You'll be amazed at how fast they grow. Choose one bean each at the beginning of the race, and see whose bean wins.

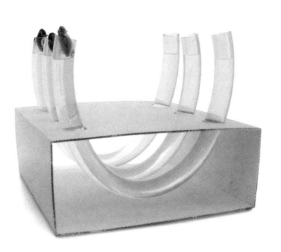

Which bit of the seed grows first?

The root starts to grow first. This anchors the plant in the ground and enables it to start drawing up water. As it lengthens, it lifts the first leaves clear of the ground so that they can start catching the sunlight as soon as possible. The first tip that appears is called the radicle, the main part that then extends is called the hypocotyl.

Where does the plant come from?

A huge oak tree grows from a tiny acorn, so where does all that mass come from? It doesn't come from the soil, that's for sure! Apart from a few nutrients, the roots only bring water into the tree. The tree actually builds itself from air using sunlight as a power source. The solid part of the tree (the bit that isn't water) is made by the tree using a process called photosynthesis, where the tree uses sunlight to unlock the carbon from carbon dioxide gas in the air.

How much does a big tree weigh?

A large, mature beech tree 30m tall, with a trunk diameter of 1m, weighs about 9 tons, 8 tons of which are above ground. The biggest giant redwood trees can weigh as much as 2,500 tons.

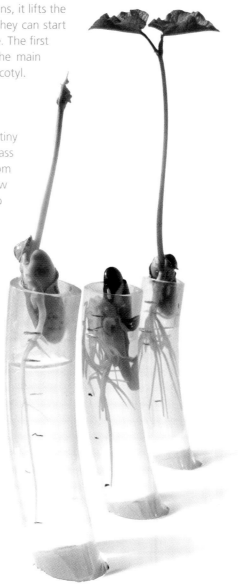

BEING THERE

Make your new place a home

Setting up a new place can be fun, but it is never easy, and it's made all the more difficult if you are leaving an established home behind. Here are ten practical tips for things you can do to speed up getting settled and help your kids to feel that they are really involved. As a dad you can make your place exciting, but you still have to have rules – while children would revert to anarchy if left to themselves, they really don't like it at all. Children need order and they need to know that the adults who care for them are in control. However, within the structure you set up, there is so much opportunity for play, and you are the best person to add that bit of sparkle to their world.

1 Involve your kids in your house hunting

Before you move into your new house or flat, try to arrange it so that you can take your children to see it, even if this means organising a special viewing. If you want your kids to feel that your new place is also their home, then they need to feel part of things as early on as possible. You may have already made the decision of where to move, but that doesn't mean that you can't involve them a bit in the process. Plan with them which room is going to be theirs or where they are going to sleep and talk with them about where you are going to put their things. However sad it is moving out of the home you have lived in together with them, there are elements of moving to a new place that are exciting. Focus on these so that your children think of the new environment positively.

2 Let your children choose their duvet cover and pillowcase

If your children are going to stay the night at your new place, make it feel like their home by letting them pick out something personal for it. Choosing something like their own bedlinen immediately makes them feel that they have something special there. A bed is an important place in a home, so encouraging your child to personalize their space in this way gives you a head start on helping them to feel settled.

3 Make a special place in your house or flat for your kids' stuff

If your house or flat isn't big enough for your children to have their own room, then put aside an area in a cupboard which they can keep as their space. If space is really tight this can be a box or part of a cupboard. Make a label with their name on it and make sure that this area stays as theirs and doesn't get filled with yours or anybody else's stuff. At the end of your time together, help them put their stuff away in their special space so that they know where it is and know that it will be there waiting for them when they come next time.

4 Buy your children something personal to keep at your house

Simple everyday things are best, because they introduce normality into a situation which is going to be strange at first. Get a couple of things like a new toothbrush or hairbrush, and if they are going to be staying the night, a set of pyjamas and a set of underclothes. These things will reduce the amount of stuff they have to bring with them from Mummy's house and will make coming to stay at your place seem much more like a home from home.

Small children will like to bring a teddy or doll – sometimes referred to as a 'transitional object' because it helps them carry a bit of their life with them. You may also want to take them out and buy them a special teddy that stays at your place ready for them when they come to stay.

5 Call their other home 'Mummy's House'

To start with you can call their other home 'Mummy's House' and your new place, 'Daddy's House' or 'Daddy's Flat'. You may still have a legal right over a part of your former marital home, but children don't understand the complicated way grown-ups have to divide up property and it is only confusing to them to try and explain this.

After a while you can call your place 'home' when they are with you and your children will understand that they can have two homes. It takes time to set up a new home but be patient and stick with it, don't expect everything to fall into place in a couple of visits. After I had been in my new flat for about a year, one of my children asked me if he could call the flat 'home', because, as he said, "We've been here for about a year now." This is when you know that all the hard work has paid off and things are really beginning to settle down.

6 Be involved in your children's social lives at every opportunity and from the earliest age possible

If your kids come to stay with you for longer than just a few hours at a time, then you should make every effort to involve yourself in a practical way with their social life. Children often have friends over to play and for tea. Once you are settled in to your new place and the routine has become established (after a couple of months or so), ask your children if they would like to have a friend over, or to go out to the cinema with you and one of their friends. If they are keen then the best way to get the ball rolling is to get the friend's mother's phone number and fix up the arrangement, parent to parent.

As your children grow up, it is important for them, and you, that you are involved in as many aspects of their normal life as possible. This won't happen if when they come to stay with you, you see that time as your exclusive time together. If you do that then as your children get older, visits to dad will eventually be seen as another separate item on their social calendar, competing with all the other things. If you treat the time they spend with you as normally as possible instead, and try to integrate it into their lives, they will see being with you as a natural extension of the things they do from week to week.

7 Play music in your house or flat

If you don't know what music your children like, ask them. When they are young, it is likely to be Disney songs or other music specifically for children, but as they grow up their tastes will change and they will get more and more into pop music. Either buy a radio or set up your CD or MP3 player to play in the background. Kids love music and they will associate their favourite tunes with happy times.

As they grow up, experiment with different music that you think they might enjoy, but don't force your favourite Bob Dylan tracks on them to the exclusion of what they like. Go with the flow, let them introduce you to new stuff, and enjoy discovering new music together.

8 Establish similar rules in your home to those they are used to at Mummy's House

Children are good at pushing boundaries, but don't think you are being kind to them if you abandon all rules when they come to stay at your home. All children need security. Provided you give them freedom to express themselves and are flexible when the occasion merits it, they will feel much better if they know that there is a structure to their lives.

Establish a bedtime and make sure that there are regular mealtimes and that your kids eat proper food when they come to stay with you. Children need consistency to know that you care about their wellbeing, even if that means having to go to bed when they would love to stay up, or not being allowed to watch a film rated much higher than their age.

Save rule-breaking for special occasions. Dads are good at taking calculated risks, so of course you can break the rules from time to time under the right circumstances – and that way it will be a real treat.

9 Add sparkle to their life at your place with things like Zebra Pops

Spice up your children's lives with fun things that don't cost anything but which add a bit of sparkle to the daily routine. For example, take one large Tupperware breakfast cereal container and alternately fill it with chocolate rice cereal and plain rice cereal and bingo, you have Zebra Pops! (Well, that's what my kids call them). Cheaper than chocolate rice cereal on their own, better for you and 100% funkier. You get an even mix of chocolate and plain rice cereal in every pour.

10 Make it fun to do even simple things, like washing hands

Another cheap way to bring light to your children's daily lives is to get foaming handwash for the bathroom. Kids love bubbles and the foaming soap makes loads, uses less soap and makes it easy for them to wash their hands and rinse them afterwards. To make it even more fun peel off the label and draw a simple picture on the pack using a permanent marker.

floating container ship PAGE 94

Epilogue

1 Sandcastle maker
2 Satellite antenna dish
3 Shower rose (holes drilled in bottom)
4 Measuring device (volume or length)
5 Plant cloche
6 Horse nosebag
7 Loudhailer (knock bottom out)
8 Small stepladder
9 Hat
10 Circle guide
11 Weapon
12 *Objet d'art*
13 Colour sample
14 Birthday present
15 Tent-peg mallet
16 Tortoise house
17 Pastry roller
18 Echo chamber
19 Small table
20 Giant's earring
21 Toilet
22 Infant's chair
23 Hazard marker
24 Investment
25 Lampshade

So how many thinking outside-the-box uses did you come up with for a bucket? Here are my 25, I bet you can think of loads more...

Have fun being with your children, making the most of the time you spend together and thinking outside-the-box in a new way, every day.

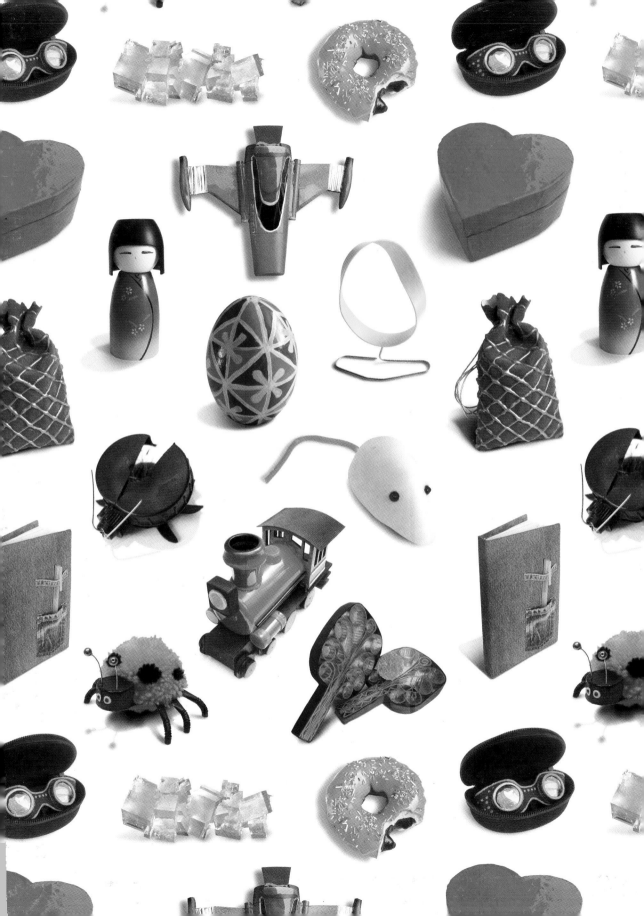